LI
A
PEACE:
INSTRUCTIONS
FOR DEVOUT SOULS
TO DISPEL THEIR DOUBTS
AND
ALLAY THEIR FEARS
By
R. P. QUADRUPANI

With an Introduction by
THE MOST REV. P. J. RYAN, D.D.,
Archbishop of Philadelphia, Pa.
1898

St Athanasius Press

ISBN-13: 978-1717072443

ISBN-10: 1717072445

St Athanasius Press
melwaller@gmail.com

Specializing in Reprinting Catholic Classics

NIHIL OBSTAT.
F. G. Holweck,
Censor Librorum.

IMPRIMATUR.
St. Louis, Mo., 1. Oct. 1897.
H. Muehlsiepen, V. G.,
Adm.

CONTENTS

PART THIRD.
Social Life.

INTRODUCTION.

God's attributes being infinite and our intellects limited and also darkened by the fall, we see these attributes only in part and "as afar off and through a glass." In contemplating His awful sanctity, we are overwhelmed with fear and forget His ineffable mercy. Our views are also greatly influenced by our natural temperaments, whether joyous or sad, and change with our environments and moods.

As the blue firmament is ever the same, so is the great God Himself—"the King of Ages immortal and invisible, without change or shadow of vicissitude." But as the clouds that hang as veils of the sanctuary are movable and variegated, now dark and gloomy and again brilliant in silver or gold, now opening into vistas of the firmament above and again closing in darkness, except when arrows of light pierce them and show their outlines, so are we variable and inconstant and need spiritual direction adapted to our peculiar wants. The naturally joyous, hopeful and sometimes presumptuous, need that wholesome fear of the Lord which is "the beginning of wisdom." The constitutionally severe, scrupulous and almost despairing, need to remember God's tender paternal character and to learn that "His mercies are above all His works." To such souls this little book must prove invaluable. Its theology is sound, as the various episcopal approbations testify. Hence its statements can be entirely trusted. The fact that it has passed through twenty editions in French is sufficient evidence of its appreciation in that country. May it continue its holy mission of light and consolation and joy in this country and act like the angelic messenger to Peter in prison, liberating the soul from the chains of doubt and despondency, illuminating her by the light of God's holy truth and bringing her out of the darksome prison into the company of the confiding, prayerful, joyous saints of God.

P. J. RYAN.

PART FIRST.
EXTERIOR PRACTICES.

I.
SPIRITUAL DIRECTION.

For it is not you who speak, but the Holy Ghost. (S. Mark, xiii, 11.)

1. It is absolutely true that in matters of conscience obedience to a spiritual director is obedience to God, for Christ has said to His ministers on earth: "He that heareth you, heareth Me." (St. Luke, x, 16.)

2. A soul possessed of this spirit of obedience can not be lost: a soul devoid of this spirit can not be saved. (St. Philip Neri.)

3. Saint Bernard says there is no need for the devil to tempt those who ignore obedience and permit themselves to be guided by their own light and deterred by their fears, for they act the devil's part towards themselves.

4. Do not fear that your director may be mistaken in what he prescribes for your guidance, or that he does not fully understand the state of your conscience because you did not explain it clearly enough to him. Such doubts cause obedience to be eluded or postponed and thus frustrate the designs of God in placing you under the direction of a prudent guide. It was the priest's duty to have questioned you further had he not fully understood you, and that he did not do so is a positive proof that he knew enough to enable him to pronounce a safe judgment. God has promised his special help to those who represent Him in the direction of souls. Is not this as-

surance enough to induce you to obey with promptness and simplicity as the Holy Scripture commands?

5. God does not show the state of our souls as clearly to us as he does to him who is to guide us in his place. You should be quite satisfied, then, if your director tells you the course you follow is the right one and that the mercy and grace of your Heavenly Father are guiding you in it. You should believe and obey him in this as in all else, for as St. John of the Cross tells us, "it betrays pride and lack of faith not to put entire confidence in what our confessor says."

6. Spiritual obedience is most needful for a Christian. Ignore, therefore, the groundless suspicion that you sin by obeying, and walk confidently in this path exempt from danger. "You sometimes fear," says St. Bonaventure, "that in obeying you act against the dictates of your conscience, whereas, on the contrary, far from incurring guilt, you really increase your merit before God."

7. We should allow obedience to regulate not only our exterior actions but likewise our mind and our will. Hence do not be satisfied with performing the works it prescribes, but let your thoughts and desires be also moulded according to its direction. In fact, it is in this interior submission that the merit of spiritual obedience essentially consists.

8. Obedience should be simple and prompt, without reservation or disquietude. Simple, because you ought not to argue about it, but decide by the one thought: I must obey; prompt, for it is God whom you obey; without reservation, because obedience extends to everything that does not violate God's law; without disquietude, because in obeying God you cannot go astray: this thought should be sufficient to drive away

all fear of doing or of having done wrong.

9. When choosing a director, be careful to select one who
has the necessary qualifications. He should be not only virtuous, but prudent, charitable and learned. St. Francis de Sales
gives the following opinion on the subject:

"Go," said Tobias to his son, when about to send him into a
strange country, 'go seek some wise man to conduct you.'
I say the same to you, Philothea. If you sincerely desire to
enter upon the way of devotion, seek a good guide to direct you therein. This advice is of the utmost importance
and necessity. Whatever one may do, says the devout Avila,
he can never be certain of fulfilling God's will, unless he
practice that humble obedience which the saints so strongly
recommend and to which they so faithfully adhere. And the
Scriptures tell us: 'A faithful friend is a strong defence: and
he that hath found him, hath found a treasure: ... a faithful
friend is the medicine of life and immortality: and they that
fear the Lord shall find one.' (Ecclesiasticus, c. VI, vv. 14-
16.)
But who can find such a friend? They that fear God, the
Wise Man answers—that is to say, those humble souls who
ardently desire their spiritual progress. Since it is so essential, then, Philothea, to have a skilful guide in the devout
life, ask God fervently to give you one according to His
Heart, and rest assured that when an angel is necessary to
you as to the young Tobias, He will give you a wise and
faithful director.

In fact, the selection once made, you should look upon your
spiritual guide more as a guardian angel than as a mere man.
You place your confidence not in him but in God, for it is
God who will lead and instruct you through his instrumen-

tality by inspiring him with the sentiments and words necessary for your guidance. Thus you may safely listen to him as to an angel sent from heaven to lead you there. To this confidence, add perfect candor. Speak quite frankly and tell him unreservedly all that is good, all that is evil in you, for the good will thus be strengthened, the evil weakened, and your soul shall thereby become firmer in its sufferings and more moderate in its consolations. Great respect should also be united with confidence and in such nice proportion that the one shall not lessen the other: let your confidence in him be such as a respectful daughter reposes in her father, your respect for him such as that with which a son confides in his mother. In a word, this friendship, though strong and tender, should be altogether sacred and spiritual in its nature.

'Choose one among a thousand,' says Avila: "among ten thousand, rather, I should say, for there are fewer than one would suppose fitted for this office of spiritual director. Charity, learning and prudence are indispensable to it, and if any one of these qualities be absent, your choice will not be unattended with danger. I repeat, ask God to inspire your selection and when you have made it thank Him sincerely, and then remain constant to your decision. If you go to God in all simplicity and with humility and confidence, you will undoubtedly obtain a favorable answer to your petition."

In conclusion, it may be well to remind you that the director and the confessor have not necessarily to be the same priest. St. Francis de Sales was the spiritual director of many persons to whom he was not the ordinary confessor. "To a director," he says, "we should reveal our entire soul, whereas to a confessor we simply accuse ourselves of our sins in order to receive absolution for them."

II.
TEMPTATIONS.

My brethren, count it all joy when ye shall fall into divers temptations. (Epist. S. Jas., Cat., c. i, v. 2.)

Now if I do that which I will not, it is no more I that do it, but sin, which dwelleth in me. (St. P., Rom., c. vii, v. 20.)

1. "If we are tempted," says the Holy Spirit, "it is a sign that God loves us." Those whom God best loves have been most exposed to temptations. "Because thou wast acceptable to God," said the angel to Tobias, "it was necessary that temptation should prove thee." (Tobias, c. xii, v. 13.)

2. Do not ask God to deliver you from temptations, but to grant you the grace not to succumb to them and to do nothing contrary to His divine will. He who refuses the combat, renounces the crown. Place all your trust in God and God will Himself do battle for you against the enemy.(1)

3. "These persistent temptations come from the malice of the devil," says St. Francis de Sales, "but the trouble and suffering they cause us come from the mercy of God. Thus, despite the will of the tempter, God converts his evil machinations into a distress which we may make meritorious. Therefore I say your temptations are from the devil and hell, but your anxiety and affliction are from God and heaven." Despise temptation, then, and open wide your soul to this suffering which God sends in order to purify you here that He may reward you hereafter.

4. "Let the wind blow," remarks the same Saint, "and do not mistake the rustling of leaves for the clashing of arms.

Be perfectly convinced that all the temptations of hell are powerless to defile a soul that does not love them. St. Paul endured terrible temptations, yet God, through love, did not deliver him from them." Look upon God as an infinitely good and tender father and believe that He only allows the devil to try His children that their merits may increase and their recompense be correspondingly greater.

5. The more persistent the temptation, the clearer it is that you have not given consent to it. "It is a good sign," says St. Francis de Sales, "when the tempter makes so much noise and commotion outside of the will, for it shows that he is not within." An enemy does not besiege a fortress that is already in his power, and the more obstinate the attack, the more certain We may be that our resistance continues.

6. Your fears lead you to believe you are defeated at the very moment you are gaining the victory. This comes from the fact that you confound feeling with consent, and, mistaking a passive condition of the imagination for an act of the will, you consider that you have yielded to the temptation because you felt it keenly.

*St. Francis de Sales, with his usual simplicity, thus describes this warring of the flesh against the spirit:

"You are right, my dear daughter. There are two women within you ... and the two children of these different mothers quarrel, and the good-for-nothing one is so bad that sometimes the good one can scarcely defend herself, and then she takes it into her head that she has been worsted and that the wicked one is braver than she. Now, surely, this is not true. The bad one is not the stronger by any means, but only slyer, more persistent and more obstinate. When she succeeds in making you weep she is delighted, because that is always just so much time lost, and she is content to make you lose time when she cannot make you lose eternity."*(2)

It is not always in our power to restrain the imagination. St. Jerome had retired into the desert and still his fancy represented to him the dances of the Roman ladies. His body was benumbed, as it were, and his blood chilled by the severity of his mortifications, and yet the flames of concupiscence encompassed and tortured his heart. During these frightful conflicts the holy anchorite suffered, but he did not sin; he was tormented but was not guilty; on the contrary, his merits were augmented in the sight of God in proportion to the intensity of the temptations.

7. The holy abbot St. Anthony was wont to say to the phantoms of his mind: I see you, but I do not look at you: I see you because it does not depend upon me that my imagination places before my eyes things I would wish not to see; I do not look at you because with my will I repulse and reject you. "It is so much the essence of sin to be voluntary," says St. Augustine, "that if not voluntary, it is not sin."

8. The attraction of the feelings towards the object presented by the imagination is at times so strong that the will seems to have been carried away and overcome by a sort of fascination. This, however, is not the case. The will suffered, but did not consent; it was attacked and wounded, but not conquered. This state of things coincides with what St. Paul says of the revolt of the flesh against the spirit and of their unceasing warfare. The soul, indeed, experiences strange sensations, but as she does not consent to them, she passes through the ordeal unsullied, just as substances coated with oil may be immersed in water without absorbing a single

drop of it.

St. Francis de Sales explains this distinction so plainly and yet so simply in one of his letters, that it may be useful to repeat the passage here: "Courage, my dear soul, I say it with great love in Jesus Christ, dear soul, courage! As long as we can exclaim resolutely, even though without feeling, My Jesus! there is no cause for alarm. Do not tell me it appears to you that you say it in a cowardly way, and only by doing great violence to yourself. It is precisely this holy violence that bears away the kingdom of heaven. Do you not see, my daughter, it is a sign that the enemy has taken everything within our fortress except the impenetrable, unconquerable tower—and that can never be lost save by wilful surrender. This tower is the free-will which, perfectly visible to the eye of God, occupies the highest and most spiritual region of the soul, dependent on none but God and oneself; and when all the other faculties are lost and in subjection to the enemy, it alone remains free to give or to refuse consent. Now, you often see souls afflicted because the enemy, occupying all the other faculties, makes therein so great a noise and confusion that they scarce can hear what this superior will says; for though it has a clearer and more penetrating voice than the inferior will, the loud, boisterous cries of the latter almost drown it: but note this well: as long as the temptation is displeasing to you, there is nothing to fear; for why should it displease you, except because you do not will it?"

9. Should it frequently happen that you have not a distinct consciousness of your success against temptation, it may be that God refuses you this satisfaction in order that, lacking this clear assurance, your knowledge may come through obedience. Therefore, when your spiritual director, after hearing your explanation, says that you have not given con-

sent, you should be satisfied with his decision and abide by it with perfect tranquillity, discarding all fear that he did not understand you aright or that you did not explain the matter sufficiently. These doubts are but fresh artifices of the devil to rob you of the merit of obedience. As has been said above, to give way to such inquietude is to offend seriously against this virtue, for all direction would thus be rendered impossible, by the failure of the penitent to recognize God Himself in the person of his director.

10. To constitute a mortal sin three conditions must co-exist. First, the matter must be weighty; secondly, the mind must have full knowledge of the guilt of the action, omission or dangerous occasion in question; and, thirdly, the will, through a criminal preference for the forbidden action, culpable omission, or proximate occasion of sin, must give full consent. These reflections should serve to reassure your mind if the fear of having committed a mortal sin disturb it, for it is very difficult for this threefold union of conditions to be effected in a God-fearing soul. However, perfect security can come, and ought to come, only from spiritual obedience.

11. In temptations against faith and purity, do not make great efforts to form acts of these virtues, but simply turn a pleading glance towards God, without speaking even to this compassionate Friend concerning the thought that afflicts you, lest thereby you root the evil suggestion more firmly. Then, without disquieting yourself, engage at once in some exterior occupation or continue what you were doing. Make no answer to the tempter, but ignore him, just as though his assault had never occurred. In this way, whilst preserving your own peace of soul, you will cover your enemy with confusion.

*The same counsel is given by St. Francis de Sales in his characteristic style:

"Do you know how God acts on these occasions? He permits the wicked maker of such wares to come and offer them to us for sale, in order that by the contempt we show for them we may testify our love for holy things. And for this is it necessary, my dear child, to feel anxious, and to change our position? No, no. It is only the devil who is prowling around your soul, raging and storming, to see if he can find an open door.... What! and you would be annoyed at that? Let the enemy storm away; only be careful on your part to keep all the entrances well fastened, and finally he will grow weary; or if he do not, God will force him to raise the siege."*

12. Though you should be assailed by temptations during your entire life time, do not be disquieted, for your merits will increase in proportion to your trials and your crown be accordingly all the brighter in heaven. The only thing necessary is to remain firm in your resolution to despise the efforts of the tempter.

"This serious trial, and so many others that have assailed you and left you troubled in mind, do not at all surprise me, since there is nothing worse. Do not worry, then, my beloved daughter. Should we allow ourselves to be swept away by the current and the storm? Let Satan rage at the door; he may knock and stamp, and clamor and howl, and do his worst, but rest assured that he can never enter our souls but through the door of our consent. Let us only keep that closed tight and often look to see that it is well secured and we need have no concern about all the rest—there is no danger."— St. Francis de Sales.

13. The most learned theologians and masters of the spiritual life agree in saying that simply to ignore a temptation is a much more effectual means to repulse it than words and acts of the contrary virtues. On this subject read attentively Chapters III. and IV. of the Introduction to a Devout Life. You will find much light and consolation in them. See also Chapter XII. of the Spiritual Combat, and Chapters VI., VII., XII., XX., XXIX., LV., and LVII. of the Third Book of the Imitation.

III.
PRAYER.

Who can persevere the whole day in the praise of God? I will suggest a help. Whatsoever thou doest do well, and thou hast praised God. (S. Aug., on Ps. xxxiv., Disc. 2.)

Oh! what do I suffer interiorly whilst with my mind I consider heavenly things; and presently a crowd of carnal thoughts interrupt me as I pray. (Imit., B. III., c. XLVIII., v. 5.)

1. We ought to love meditation and should make it often on the Passion of our divine Lord, striving above all to derive therefrom fruits of humility, patience and charity.

2. If you experience great dryness in your meditations or other prayers, do not feel distressed and conclude that God has turned His Face away from you. Far from it. Prayer said with aridity is usually the most meritorious. *It is quite a common error to confound the value of prayer with its sensible results, and the merit acquired with the satisfaction experienced. The facility and sweetness you may have in prayer are favors from God and for which you will have to account to him: hence the result is not merit but debt. (Read the Imitation, B. II, c. IX.)* The very fact that we derive less gratification from such prayer, makes it all the more pleasing to God, because we are thus suffering for love of him. Let us call to mind at such times that our Lord prayed without consolation throughout his bitter agony.

*"All this trouble comes from self-love and from the good opinion we have of ourselves. If our hearts do not melt with tenderness, if we have no relish or sensible feeling in prayer, if we do not enjoy great interior sweetness during medita-

tion, we are at once overwhelmed with sadness: if we find difficulty in doing good, if some obstacle is opposed to our pious designs, we give way to disquietude and are eager to conquer all this and to be free from it. Why? Undoubtedly because we love consolations, our own comfort, our own convenience. We wish to pray immersed in sweetness, and to be virtuous that we may eat sugar; and we do not contemplate our Saviour Jesus Christ, who, prone upon the ground, is covered with a sweat of blood caused by the intense conflict He feels interiorly between the repugnances of the inferior portion of his soul and the resolutions of the superior."*—St. Francis de Sales.

*The same teaching is given by another great master of the spiritual life:

"We frequently seek the gratification and consolation of self-love in the testimony we desire to render to ourselves. Thus we are disturbed about our lack of sensible fervor, whereas in reality we never pray so well as when we are tempted to think we are not praying at all. We fear to pray badly then, but we should fear rather to give way to the vexation of our cowardly nature, to a philosophical infidelity, which ever wishes to demonstrate to itself its own operations—in fine, to an impatient desire to see and to feel in order to console ourselves.

There is no penance more bitter than this state of pure faith without sensible support. Hence I conclude that it is freer than any other from illusion. Strange temptation! to seek impatiently for sensible consolation through fear of not being sufficiently penitent! Ah! Why not rather accept as a penance the deprivation of that consolation we are so tempted to seek?"*—Fénelon.

3. You will sometimes imagine that at prayer your soul is not in the presence of God and that only your body is in the church, like the statues and candelabras that adorn the altars. Think, then, that you share with those inanimate objects the honor of serving as ornaments for the house of God, and that in the presence of your Creator even this humble rôle should seem glorious to you.

"You tell me that you cannot pray well. But what better prayer could there be than to represent to God again and again, as you are doing, your nothingness and misery? The most touching appeal beggars can make is merely to expose to us their deformities and necessities. But there are times when you cannot even do this much, you say, and that you remain there like a statue. Well, even that is better than nothing. Kings and princes have statues in their palaces for no other purpose than that they may take pleasure in looking at them: be satisfied then to fulfil the same office in the presence of God, and when it so pleases Him He will animate the statue."—St. Francis de Sales.

4. When you have not consciously or voluntarily yielded to distractions, do not stop to find what may have been their cause, or to discover if you have in any way given occasion to them. This would be simply to weary and disquiet yourself unprofitably. From whatever direction they come, you can convert them into a source of merit by casting yourself into the arms of the Divine Mercy. St. Francis de Sales when asked how he prayed, replied: "I cannot say it too often—I receive peacefully whatever the Lord sends me. If he consoles me, I kiss the right hand of his mercy; if I am dry and distracted, I kiss the left hand of his justice." This method is the only good one, for as the same Saint says: "He who truly loves prayer, loves it for the love of God: and he who loves

it for the love of God, wishes to experience in it naught but what God is pleased to send him." Now, whatever you may experience in prayer, is precisely what God wills.

5. St. Francis de Sales teaches us that merely to keep ourselves peacefully and tranquilly in the presence of God, without other desire or pretension than to be near him and to please him, is of itself an excellent prayer. "Do not exhaust yourself," he says, "in making efforts to speak to your dear Master, for you are speaking to Him by the sole fact that you remain there and contemplate Him."

*"Remember that the graces and favors of prayer do not come from earth but from heaven and therefore that no effort of ours can acquire them, although, it is true, we must dispose ourselves for their reception diligently, yet withal humbly and tranquilly. We ought to keep our hearts wide open and await the blessed dew from heaven. The following consideration should never be forgotten when we go to prayer, namely, that we draw near to God and place ourselves in His presence principally for two reasons. The first is to render to God the honor and the homage we owe Him, and this can be done without God speaking to us or we to Him, for the duty is fulfilled by acknowledging that He is our Creator and we are His vile creatures, and by remaining before Him, prostrate in spirit, awaiting His commands. The second reason is to speak to God and to listen to Him when He speaks to us by His inspirations and the interior movements of grace.... Now, one or other of these two advantages can never fail to be derived from prayer. If, then, we can speak to our Lord, let us do so in praise and supplication: if we are unable to speak, let us remain in his presence notwithstanding, offering him our silent homage; he will see us there, our patience will touch him and our silence will plead with him and win

his favor. Another time, to our utter astonishment, he will take us by the hand, and converse with us, and make a hundred turns with us in his garden of prayer. And even should he never do this, still let us be content to know it is our duty to be in his retinue, and that it is a great favor and a greater honor for us that he suffers us in his presence.

In this way we do not force ourselves to speak to God, for we know that merely to remain close to him is as useful, nay, perhaps more useful to us, though it may be less to our liking. Therefore when you draw near to our Lord speak to him if you can; if you cannot, stay there, let him see you, and do not be anxious about anything else.... Take courage, then, tell your Saviour you will not leave him even should he never grant you any sensible sweetness; tell him that you will remain before him until he has given you his blessing."*—St. Francis de Sales.

6. The same Saint gives further valuable advice as follows: "Many persons fail to make a distinction between the presence of God in their souls and the consciousness of this adorable presence, between faith and the sensible feeling of faith. This shows a great want of discernment. When they do not realize God's presence dwelling within them, they suppose He has withdrawn himself through some fault of theirs. This is an ignorant and hurtful error. A man who endures martyrdom for love of God does not think actually and exclusively of God but much of his own sufferings; and yet the absence of this feeling of faith does not deprive him of the great merit due to his faith and the resolutions it caused him to make and to keep."

7. Your vocal prayers should be few in number but said with great fervor. The strength derived from food does not depend

upon the quantity taken but upon its being well digested. Far better one Our Father or one Psalm said with devout attention than entire rosaries and long offices recited hurriedly and with restless eagerness.

8. If you feel whilst saying vocal prayers—those not of obligation—that God invites you to meditate, gently and promptly follow this divine impulse. You may be sure that in doing so you make an exchange most profitable to yourself and agreeable to God from whom the inspiration comes.

9. Prepare yourself for prayer by peaceful recollection and begin it without agitation or uneasiness. St. Francis de Sales has this to say on the subject: "Some little time before you are going to pray, calm and compose your heart, and be hopeful of doing well; for if you begin without hope and already devoid of relish, you will find it difficult to regain an appetite.... The disquiet you experience in prayer, accompanied by great eagerness to discover some object that can fix and satisfy your thoughts, is of itself sufficient to prevent you finding what you seek. When a thing is searched for with too great eagerness, one may have his hands or his eyes almost upon it a hundred times and yet fail to perceive it. This vain and useless anxiety in regard to prayer can result in nothing but weariness of mind, and this in turn produces coldness and apathy in your soul."

10. Be careful not to overburden yourself with too many prayers, either mental or vocal. As soon as you feel uncontrollable weariness or distaste, postpone your prayers, if possible, and seek relief in some pleasant pastime, or conversation, or in any other innocent diversion. This advice is given by St. Thomas and other learned Fathers of the Church and is of the utmost importance. Follow it conscientiously,

for lassitude of mind begets coldness and a kind of spiritual stupor.

11. Never repeat a prayer, even should you have said it with many distractions. You cannot imagine the innumerable difficulties in which you may become entangled by the habit of repeating your prayers. Therefore I beg of you not to do it. *In St. Ignatius' time there was a certain religious of the Society of Jesus who was a victim of this kind of scruple. The recital of the daily Office always kept him much longer than was necessary because he would repeat again and again and for hours at a time any passage that he suspected had not been said with sufficient attention. St. Ignatius tried to correct him by various means, but in vain. At length the thought occurred that one scruple might be cured by another. He therefore commanded the poor Jesuit, under pain of sin and in virtue of religious obedience, to close his breviary every day at the end of a specified time, this being just enough to allow him to read the Office through once and rather quickly. The first day the religious was obliged to stop before he had half finished. This caused him such intense regret that ere long the fear of not being able to say the entire Office made him contract the habit of finishing it within the allotted time.* Begin your prayer with the desire of being very recollected. This is all that is necessary. "A desire has the same value in the sight of God as a good work", says St. Gregory the Great, "when the accomplishment of it does not depend upon our will." During these involuntary distractions God withdraws the sensible feeling of His presence, but His love remains in the depths of our hearts. St. Theresa, in the midst of dryness and distractions, was wont to say: "If I am not praying I am at least doing penance." I should say: you are doing both the one and the other: you do penance by all that you are suffering, you pray by the desire and intention you

24

have to do so.

12. You should never repeat a prayer nor a point in your meditation even if you have had in the inferior portion of your soul ideas and feelings at variance with the words pronounced by your lips or with the sentiments you wished to excite in your heart. Nay, do not be induced to do it, even were these ideas and feelings injurious to God. Under such conditions, be careful not to give way to anxiety and agitation and do not try to make reparation for an imaginary offence. Continue your prayer in peace as if nothing had disturbed it, not taking the trouble to notice these dogs that come from the devil and that can bark around you while you pray in order to distract you, if may be, but that cannot bite you unless you let them. *"This temptation should be treated exactly the same as temptations of the flesh: do not dispute with it at all, rather imitate the children of Israel who made no attempt to break the bones of the paschal lamb but cast them into the fire. You need not answer the enemy, nor even pretend to hear what he says. Let the wretch clamor at the door as much as he wants to, it is not even necessary to call: Who is there? What you tell me is no doubt true, you say, but he annoys me and the uproar he makes prevents those within from hearing one another speak. That makes no difference. Have patience, prostrate yourself before God and remain at his feet. He will understand from your very attitude, although you utter no words, that you are his and that you crave his help. Above all, however, keep yourself well within and do not on any account open the door, either to see who it is, or to drive the importunate fellow away. Eventually he will tire of shouting and will leave you in peace."*(3) St. Augustine says that the devil is a formidable giant to those who fear him, but only a miserable dwarf to those who despise him.

13. Should it happen that the whole time given to prayer be passed in rejecting temptations or in recalling your mind from its wanderings, and you do not succeed in giving birth to a single devout thought or sentiment, St. Francis de Sales is authority for saying that your prayer is nevertheless all the more meritorious from the fact of its being so unsatisfactory to you. It makes you more like to our divine Lord when he prayed in the Garden of Gethsemani and on Mount Calvary. "Better to eat bread without sugar, than sugar without bread. We should seek the God of consolations, not the consolations of God: and in order to possess God in heaven, we must now suffer with him and for him."

"When your mind wanders or gives way to distractions, gently recall it and place it once more close to its Divine Master. If you should do nothing else but repeat this during the whole time of prayer, your hour would be very well spent and you would perform a spiritual exercise most acceptable to God."—St. Francis de Sales.

14. It is well to bear in mind that in commanding us to pray always our Saviour did not mean actual prayer, as that would be an impossibility. The desire to glorify God by all our actions suffices for the rigorous fulfilment of this precept, if this desire be habitual and permanent. "You pray often," says St. Augustine, "if you often have a desire to pay homage to God by your actions: you pray always if you always have this desire, no matter how you may be otherwise employed."

*"Need we be surprised that St. Augustine often assures us that the whole Christian life is but one long, continual tending of our hearts towards that eternal justice for which we sigh here below? Our only happiness consists in ever thirst-

ing for it, and this thirst is in itself a prayer; consequently if we always desire this justice, we pray always. Do not think it necessary to pronounce a great many words and to struggle much with one's self in order to pray. To pray is to ask God that his will may be done, to form some good desire, to raise the heart to God, to long for the riches he promises us, to sigh over our miseries and the danger we are in of displeasing him by violating His holy law. Now this requires neither science nor method nor reasoning; one can pray without any distinct thought; no head-work is necessary; only a moment of time and a loving effusion of the heart are needed; and even this moment may be simultaneously occupied with something else, for so great is God's condescension to our weakness that he permits us to divide it when necessary between him and creatures. Yes, during this moment you can continue what you were doing: it is sufficient to offer to God your most ordinary occupations, or to perform them with the general intention of glorifying him. This is the continual prayer required by St. Paul ... thought by many devout persons to be impracticable, but in reality very easy for those who know that the best of all prayers is to do everything with a pure intention, and frequently to renew the desire to perform all our actions for God and in accordance with his divine will."—Fénelon.*

15. You should never omit or neglect the duties of your state of life in order to say certain self-imposed prayers. These duties are a substitute for prayers and are equally efficacious, St. Thomas teaches, for obtaining the graces you stand in need of and which are promised to those who ask them properly. It is even more meritorious to perform some work for the love of God, to whom we offer it, than merely to raise the soul to Him by actual prayer.

"Every person is bound to observe strictly the duties of his particular calling. Whoever fails to do this, although he should raise the dead to life, is guilty of sin and should the sin be grave deserves damnation if he die therein. For example, bishops are obliged to make a visitation of their diocese in order to console and instruct their flock and to rectify whatever may be amiss. If I, a bishop, neglect this duty I shall be lost even though I spend my entire time in prayer and fast all my life."—St. Francis de Sales.

16. Make frequent use of the prayers called ejaculations,—which are short and loving aspirations that raise the soul to its Creator. According to St. Francis de Sales, ejaculations can in case of necessity replace all other prayers, whereas all other prayers cannot supply for the omission of ejaculations.

"Acquire the habit of making frequent ejaculations. They are sighs of love that dart upwards to God to sue for His aid and succor. It will greatly facilitate this custom if you keep in mind the point of your morning's meditation that you liked best and ponder it over during the day. In sickness let pious ejaculations take the place of all other prayers."—St. Francis de Sales.

17. Ejaculatory prayers can be made at all times, wherever we are or whatever we may be doing. They might be compared to those aromatic pastilles, which we may always have about us and take from time to time to strengthen the stomach and please the palate. Ejaculations have a like effect on the soul by refreshing and fortifying it.

18. The monks of old, of whom St. Augustine speaks, could not say long prayers, obliged as they were to earn their bread by daily toil. Ejaculatory prayers, therefore, took the place of

all others for them, and it may be said that although laboring unceasingly they prayed continually.

19. I cannot too earnestly urge you to accustom yourself to the profitable and easy practice of making frequent ejaculations. It is far preferable to saying many other vocal prayers, for these when too numerous are apt to employ the lips only rather than to reanimate and enlighten the soul.

20. St. Theresa's opinion is that the body should be in a comfortable position when we pray, as otherwise it is difficult for the mind to pay the proper attention to prayer and to the presence of God. Do not then fatigue your body by remaining too long prostrate or kneeling: the important thing is that the soul should humble itself before God in sentiments of respect, confidence and love.

Read Chap. XIII, Part II, of the Introduction to a Devout Life.

IV.
PENANCE.

A sacrifice to God is an afflicted spirit; a contrite and humble heart, O God, thou wilt not despise. (Ps. L., 19.)

I. According to the teaching of St. Thomas there are three ways of doing penance, namely, fasting, prayer, and alms-deeds—either corporal or spiritual. Therefore you must not suppose you are prevented from doing penance when not allowed to subject your body to severe fasts and painful mortifications. The other two penitential works, prayer and almsgiving, can in this case take the place of corporal austerities in the fulfilment of the Christian duty of penance. Observe also that it is not in accordance with the spirit of the laws of God and of his Church, which prescribe fasting, to injure your health thereby, nor to hinder the accomplishment of the duties of your state of life.

2. Labor, sickness, disappointments, reverse of fortune, dryness in prayer, all these when accepted with resignation are penitential works, such, too, as are the more agreeable to God from their being so distasteful to ourselves. All virtues may be divided into two great classes, active and passive. The characteristic of the active virtues is to do good, of the passive, to endure evil. Now the virtues of the second class are more meritorious and less perilous. In the active virtues nature can have a large share, and a dangerous self-complacency, or satisfaction in their effects, may easily glide into them. This danger is less to be feared in the practice of the passive virtues, especially when the sufferings are not of our own choosing but come to us direct from the hand of God.

3. St. Jerome teaches that when the devil cannot turn a soul

away from the love of virtue, he tries to urge it to excessive mortification, in order that it may thus become exhausted and lose the vigor indispensable to its spiritual progress. Numbers of devout people have fallen into this snare.

4. "I charge you," says St. Francis de Sales, "to preserve your health carefully, for God exacts this of you, and to husband your strength so as to employ it in his service. It is even better to save more than the requisite amount of strength than to reduce it too much, for we can always lessen it at will, whereas, once lost, it is no easy matter to regain it." Therefore give your body the nourishment it needs to maintain its strength and health.

5. We learn from Cassian and St. Thomas that in a celebrated conference held by the holy Abbot St. Anthony with the most learned religious of Egypt, it was decided that of all virtues moderation is the most useful, as it guards and preserves all the others. It is owing to the lack of this essential moderation in their devotional exercises and mortifications that many persons whilst seeking holiness find only ill health. As a consequence they eventually abandon the path of perfection, judging it impracticable because they have attempted to walk in it bound with fetters.

6. St. Augustine makes the following apt comparison, which you can look upon as a good rule in this matter: "The body is a poor invalid confided to the charity of the soul, the soul being commissioned to give it such assistance as it requires. Hunger, thirst, fatigue, are its habitual ailments; let the soul then charitably apply to them the needful remedies, provided these be always within the bounds of moderation and prudence." He who acts in this way fulfils a duty of obedience to his Creator.

7. From these various opinions it is easy to see how false are certain maxims met with in some ascetical works: for example, that it is of small consequence if one should shorten his life by ten or fifteen years in order to save his soul. If this were true, a much surer way would be to secure a still speedier death, and see to what that would lead. No: it is not permissible in ordinary practice to impose upon ourselves arbitrarily any kind of mortification that would directly tend to shorten life. "To kill one's self with a single blow," says St. Jerome, "or to kill one's self little by little—I make but slight distinction between these two crimes." Life, health and strength are blessings that have been given us in trust, and we cannot lawfully dispose of them as though they belonged to us absolutely.

8. The example of those saints who practised extraordinary penances deserves our sincere admiration, but it is not in these exterior acts that we should try to imitate them; to do this would necessitate being as holy as they were. Duplicate their miracles also, then, if you can. "If we had to copy the saints in everything they did," says St. Frances de Chantal, "it would be necessary to spend our life in a horrible cave like St. John Climachus, or on top of a pillar as St. Simon Stylites did, to live several weeks without other nourishment than the Holy Eucharist like St. Catharine of Sienna, or to eat but a single ounce of food each day as St. Aloysius did." Aspirations to imitate the saints in what is extraordinary are the effect of secret pride and not of genuine virtue.

*The French translator of these Instructions had a conversation in Rome with the learned and pious Jesuit, Rev. Father Rozaven, on this subject. Speaking of the extraordinary fasts and mortifications of St. Ignatius, Father Rozaven said:

"Do not let us confound cause and effect. It is not because he did these things that Ignatius became a saint: on the contrary, it is because he was already a saint that it was possible and permissible for him to do them." In truth every act that exceeds human strength is an act of presumption unless it be the result of a special inspiration, and the Church approves it only if she recognizes this divine impulse which alone can authorize a deviation from the general rule. It is owing to such an exception that she venerates among those who suffered for the faith Saint Theodora, Saint Pomposa, Saint Flora and Saint Denys, notwithstanding the fact that they violated the law which forbids any one to seek martyrdom. The same spirit influenced her in sanctioning the voluntary death of Sampson and of Saint Appolonia, who might be called pious suicides were it allowable to connect two such contradictory words.—Read Chap. XXIII, Part III. of the Introduction to a Devout Life.*

V.
CONFESSION.

I said: I will confess against myself my injustice to the Lord, and thou hast forgiven the wickedness of my sin. (Ps. XXXI, 5.)

But if any man sin, we have an advocate with the Father, Jesus Christ the Just. (1st Epist. St. John, c. II, v. 1.)

Whose sins ye shall forgive, they are forgiven them: and whose ye shall retain, they are retained. (St. John, c. XX. v. 23.)

1. The sacrament of penance is a sacrament of mercy. We should therefore approach it with confidence and in peace. Saint Francis de Sales assures us that for those who go to confession once a week a quarter of an hour is enough for the examination of conscience, and a still shorter time for exciting contrition. Not even this much is necessary, he adds, for those who confess more frequently.

2. Faults omitted in confession either because they were forgotten or because they seemed too trivial to mention, are nevertheless effaced by the absolution. St. Francis de Sales has this to say on the subject: "You must not feel worried if you cannot remember your sins when preparing for confession, for it is incredible that any one who often examines her conscience would overlook or be unable to recall such faults as are important. Neither should you be so keenly anxious to mention every minute imperfection, every trifling fault; it is enough to speak of these to our Lord, with a sigh of regret and a humble heart, whenever you remark them." And do not imagine in consequence that you are guilty of secret sins

which you are hiding from your confessor. This fear is an artifice made use of by the devil to disturb your peace of mind.

"You must not be so anxious to tell everything, nor to run to your superiors to make a great ado over each little thing that troubles you and that will, perhaps, be forgotten in a quarter of an hour. We must learn to bear with generosity these trifles which we cannot remedy, for ordinarily they are only the consequences of our imperfect nature. That your will, feelings, and desires are so inconstant; that you are at one time moody, at another cheerful; that you now have a wish to speak, and presently feel the greatest aversion to do so; and a thousand similar insignificant matters are infirmities to which we are naturally prone and will be subject to as long as we live.... It is needless to accuse yourself in confession of those fleeting thoughts that like gnats swarm around you, or of the disgust and aversion you feel in the observance of your vows and devotional exercises, for these things are not sins, they are only inconveniences, annoyances."—St. Francis de Sales.

3. Rest assured that the more closely you examine your conscience the less you will discover that is worth the trouble of telling. Moreover, you must remember that too long an examen fatigues the mind and cools the fervor of the heart.

4. To those who in their confessions are inclined to confuse involuntarily movements with sins, Saint Francis de Sales gives the following useful advice: "You tell me that when you have experienced a strong feeling of anger, or have had any other temptation, you are always uneasy if you do not confess it. When you are not sure that you have given consent to it, I assure you it is unnecessary to mention it except it may be in spiritual conference, and then not by way of ac-

cusation, but to obtain advice how to behave another time in like circumstances. For if you say: I accuse myself of having had movements of violent anger for two days, but I did not give way to them, you are telling your virtues, not your sins. A doubt comes into my mind, though, that I may have committed some fault during the temptation. You must consider maturely if this doubt have any foundation in fact, and if so, speak of the matter in confession with all simplicity; otherwise it is better not to mention it, as you would do so only for your own satisfaction. Even should this silence cost you some pain, you must endure it as you would any other to which you can apply no remedy."

5. "Omit from your confessions"—we again quote the same Saint—"those superfluous accusations which so many persons make merely through habit: I have not loved God sufficiently; I have not prayed with enough fervor; I have not loved my neighbor as much as I should; I have not received the Sacraments with all the reverence due to them; and others of a like nature. You will readily see the reason for this. It is that in speaking thus you tell nothing particular that would make known to the confessor the state of your conscience, and because the most perfect man living, as well as all the saints in Paradise might say the same things were they making a confession."

6. Those who go to confession frequently should always bear in mind what the saintly director says in addition: "We are not obliged to confess our venial sins, but if we do so it must be with a firm resolution to correct them, otherwise it is an abuse of the sacrament to mention them."

7. After confession keep your soul in peace, and be on your guard—this is a point of cardinal importance—against giv-

ing access to any fear about the validity of the sacrament, either as regards the examination of conscience, the contrition, or anything else whatsoever. These fears are suggestions of the devil whose aim it is to instil bitterness into a sacrament of consolation and love.

"After confession is not the time to examine ourselves to find if we have told all our sins. We should rather remain attentively and in peace near our Lord, with whom We have just been reconciled, and thank Him for His great mercy. Nor is it necessary subsequently to search out what we may have forgotten. We must tell simply all that comes to mind; after that we need think no more about it."—St. Francis de Sales.

8. It is essential to be sorry for our sins—it is not essential to be troubled about them. Repentance is an effect of love of God, anxiety is an effect of self-love. In the midst of the keenest and most sincere repentance we can still thank God that He has not permitted us to become yet more culpable. Let us promise Him a solid amendment, relying for success solely upon the assistance of divine grace; and should we fall again a hundred times a day, let us never cease to renew the promise and the hope. God can in an instant raise up from the very stones children to Abraham and exalt the most corrupt natures to the highest degree of sanctity. At times He does so, but usually it is His will that we long continue to bear the burden of our infirmity: let us not then lose our trust in Him, nor mistake a state of trial for a state of reprobation.

*God has, indeed, on some occasions cured sinners instantaneously and without leaving in them any trace of their previous maladies. Such, for instance, was the case with the Magdalen. In a moment her soul was changed from a sink of corruption into a well-spring of perfection, never again to be contaminated by sin. But, on the other hand, in several of the beloved disciples this same God allowed many marks of their evil inclinations to remain for some time after their conversion, and this for their greater good. Witness Saint Peter, who, even after the divine call, was guilty of various imperfections and once fell totally and miserably by the triple denial of his Lord and Master.

"Solomon says there is no one more insolent than a servant who has suddenly become mistress.(4) A soul that after a long slavery to its passions should in a moment subjugate them completely, would be in great danger of becoming a prey to pride and vanity. This dominion must be gained little by little, step by step; it cost the saints long years of labor to acquire it. Hence the necessity of having patience with every one, but first of all with yourself."—St. Francis de Sales.*

*There is no sight more pleasing to Heaven than to witness the persevering and determined struggle of a soul which, throughout, remains united to God by a sincere desire and a firm resolution not to offend him—and maintaining this struggle calmly and patiently even when it is to all appearance fruitless. Such a soul, resigned to retain its defects if it is God's will, yet determined notwithstanding to fight against them relentlessly, is more precious in the eyes of God than if the practice of virtue were easy for it and it were in peaceful possession of spiritual gifts. Labor, then, in the presence of your heavenly Father; struggle on with strength and courage; but do not be too desirous of success, for when this craving for self-satisfaction is excessive it is sure to be accompanied by vexation and impatience.

"Evil things must not be desired at all," says Saint Francis de Sales, "nor good things immoderately." And elsewhere:

38

"I entreat of you, love nothing too ardently, not even the virtues, for these we sometimes forfeit by exceeding the bounds of moderation." And again: "Why is it that if we happen to fall into some imperfection or sin we are surprised at ourselves and become disquieted and impatient? Undoubtedly it is because we thought there was some good in us, and that we were resolute and strong. Consequently when we find this is not the case, that we have tripped and fallen to the earth, we are anxious, annoyed and troubled; whereas if we realized what we truly are, in place of being astonished at seeing ourselves down, we should wonder rather how we ever remain erect."

"We should labor, therefore, without any uneasiness as to results. God requires efforts on our part, but not success. If we combat with perseverance, nothing daunted by our defeats, these very defeats will be worth as much to us as victories, and even more. But beware!—there is a rock here! If this conflict is not undertaken in perfectly good faith, we will try to deceive ourselves as to the genuineness of our efforts by calling the cowardice which caused us to refuse the battle a defeat, and by dignifying with the name of trial the results of our own effeminacy and sloth."*

9. Contrition is essentially an act of the will by which we detest our past sins and resolve not to commit them in future. Hence sighs, tears, sensible sorrow are not necessary elements of true contrition. Contrition can even attain that degree of disinterested perfection which suffices for the justification of a sinner, in the midst of the greatest dryness and an apparent insensibility. Therefore never allow yourself to be disturbed by the want of sensible sorrow.

10. Do not make violent efforts to excite your soul to con-

trition, for these only have the effect of producing anxiety, weariness and oppression of mind. On the contrary seek to become very calm; say lovingly to God that you wish sincerely you had never offended Him and that with the assistance of His grace you will never offend Him more—that is contrition. True contrition is a product of love, and love acts in a calm.

11. "An act of contrition," says St. Francis de Sales, "is the work of a moment." Cast a rapid glance at yourself to see and detest your sins, and another towards God to promise Him amendment and to express a hope of obtaining His assistance in keeping this promise. David, one of the most contrite penitents that ever lived, expressed his act of contrition in a single word: Peccavi—I have sinned, and by that one word he was justified.

"You ask how an act of contrition can be made in a short time? I answer that a very good one can be made in almost no time. Nothing more is needed than to prostrate oneself before God in a spirit of humility and of sorrow for having offended Him."—St. Francis de Sales.

12. You say you would wish to have contrition but cannot succeed in feeling it. Saint Francis de Sales replies: "The ability to wish is a great power with God, and you thus have contrition by the simple fact that you wish to have it. You do not feel it indeed at the moment, but neither do you see nor feel a fire covered with ashes, nevertheless the fire exists." The immoderate desire of sensible sorrow comes from self-love and self-complacency. A sorrow that satisfies only God is not sufficient for us, we wish it to satisfy us also; we like to find in our sensibility a flattering and reassuring testimony of our love of good.

13. If God does not grant you the enjoyment of sensible sorrow, it is in order that you may gain the merit of obedience, which should suffice to reassure you as to your perfect reconciliation. Believe therefore with humility, obey with courage, and you will earn a twofold reward. The greatest saints have at times believed they had neither contrition nor love, but in the midst of this darkness of the understanding, their will followed the torch of obedience with heroic submission.

14. Do not conclude that you lack contrition or that your confessions are defective, because you fall again into the same faults. It is very essential to make a distinction in regard to relapses. Those that are the offspring of a perverse will which has preserved an affection for certain venial sins, takes pleasure and wishes to take pleasure in them,—these should not be tolerated; we must vigorously attack them at the very root and not allow ourselves any respite until they are utterly exterminated. But those relapses that proceed from inadvertence, from surprise notwithstanding constant vigilance, from the infirmity and frailty of our nature, to these we shall remain partially subject until our last breath. "It will be doing very well," says Saint Francis de Sales, "if we get free of certain faults a quarter of an hour before our death." And elsewhere: "We are obliged not only to bear with the failings of our neighbor, but likewise with our own and to be patient at the sight of our imperfections." We must try to correct ourselves, but we should do it tranquilly and without anxiety. We cannot become angels before the proper time.

*"You complain that you still have many faults and failings notwithstanding your desire for perfection and a pure love of God. I assure you that it is impossible to be entirely divested of self whilst we are here below. We shall always be

41

obliged to bear ourselves about with us until God transfers us to heaven; and whilst we do this we carry something that is of no value. It is necessary, therefore, to have patience, and not to expect to cure ourselves in a day of the numerous bad habits contracted through past carelessness in regard to our spiritual welfare. Pray do not look here, there and everywhere: look only at God and yourself; you will never see God devoid of goodness, nor yourself without wretchedness and that wretchedness the object of God's goodness and mercy."—St. Francis de Sales. (After the examination of conscience read the Following of Christ, B. III., Chap. XX.)*

Fénelon speaks in the same tone: "You should never be surprised or discouraged at your faults. You must bear with them patiently yet without flattering yourself or sparing correction. Treat yourself as you would another. As soon as you find you have committed a fault make an interior act of self-condemnation, turn to God to receive a penance, and then tell your fault with simplicity to your director. Begin over again to do well as though it were the first time, and do not grow weary if you have to make a fresh start every day. Nothing is more touching to the Sacred Heart of Jesus than this humble and patient courage. We should not be cast down if we have many temptations and even commit numerous faults. 'Virtue,' says the Apostle, 'is made perfect in infirmity.'(5) Spiritual progress is effected less by sensible devotion, relish and spiritual consolations, than by means of interior humiliation and frequent recourse to God."

15. Habitually add to your confession some general accusation of all the sins of your past life, or of such of them as occasion you most remorse. Say, for example, I accuse myself of sins against purity, or charity, or temperance. You

thus preclude the possibility of there being lack of sufficient matter for the validity of the Sacrament.

16. Banish from your mind the dread of having omitted any sins in either your general or ordinary confessions, or of not having explained their circumstances clearly enough. The learned theologian Janin sets forth the following rules on the subject: The Church, the interpreter of the will of Jesus Christ, requires sacramental integrity in confession, and not material integrity. The former consists in the confession of all the sins we can remember after a sufficient examination, the duration of which should be regulated by the actual state of the conscience. Material integrity would require a rigorously complete accusation of all the sins we have committed with their number and circumstances, without the slightest omission. Now sacramental integrity may be reasonably exacted since it exceeds no one's ability; whilst material integrity, on the contrary, could not be exacted without the sacrament becoming an impossibility; for, no matter how carefully we make our examination of conscience, some sin, or some detail in regard to number or circumstance, will always escape us. In a word, all that the Church demands of the faithful is a sincere and humble avowal of every sin that can be brought to mind after a suitable examen: for the rest, she intends good will to supply for any defect of memory.

Do not be uneasy because you fail to remember all your failings in order to tell them in confession. This is unnecessary, because as you often fall almost without being aware of it, so you often get up again without perceiving it; just as in the passage you quote it is not said that the just man sees or feels himself fall seven times a day, but simply that he falls seven times a day: in like manner he gets up again without noticing particularly that he has done so. Hence have no anxiety about this, but frankly and humbly confess whatever you remember, and commit the rest to the tender mercies of him who puts his hand under those who fall without malice that they may not be bruised, and raises them up again so gently and swiftly that they scarcely realize they had fallen.—St. Francis de Sales.

17. By a diligent examination of conscience you have thoroughly satisfied all the requirements for sacramental integrity; therefore banish whatever doubts and fears may come to beset you, for they are nothing but temptations.

18. Should you suspect that you failed to fulfil these requirements owing to not having been particular enough about your examination of conscience, you may feel sure that your confessor has by prudent interrogations supplied for whatever may have been wanting on your part. And if he did not question you further it was due to the fact that he understood clearly enough the nature of your sins and the state of your soul, and this is the object of sacramental accusation.

19. How great then is the error of those poor souls who wish continually to make their general confessions over again, either through fear of incomplete examination or of insufficient sorrow; and how blameworthy the weak complaisance of those confessors who offer no opposition to their doing so! If such fears were to be listened to, every one would be obliged to pass his entire life in making and repeating general confessions, for they would incessantly spring up afresh and even the greatest saints would not be exempt from them. A sacrament of consolation and love would thus be transformed into a perfect torture for the soul—an heretical perversion anathematized by the Council of Trent.

"I have found in your general confession all the marks of a sincere, good and earnest confession. Never have I heard one that more thoroughly satisfied me. You may rely on this, for in these matters I speak very plainly. However, if you really omitted something that ought to have been told, consider if you did so consciously and voluntarily, in which case, if it was a mortal sin or you thought it one at the time, you would undoubtedly have to make the confession over again. But if it were only a venial sin, or though mortal you omitted it out of forgetfulness or some defect of memory, have no scruples; for at my soul's peril, I assure you there is no obligation to repeat your confession. It will be quite sufficient to mention the matter to your ordinary confessor. I will answer for this."—St. Francis de Sales.

20. It is the teaching of the saints and doctors of the Church that when a general confession has been made with a sincere and upright intention and with a desire to change one's life, the penitent should remain in peace in regard to it, and not make it over again under any pretext whatsoever. Those who do otherwise recall to their memory things that should be banished from it, and increase the trouble of their soul by a too eager desire to purify it. For, as Saint Philip de Neri so well expresses it: the harder we sweep, the more dust we raise.

21. Remember, in conclusion, that according to the common opinion of the saints, the fear of sin is no longer salutary when it becomes excessive.

VI.
HOLY COMMUNION.

Unless ye eat the flesh of the Son of Man, and drink His blood, ye shall not have life in you. (St. John, c. vi., v. 54.)

And he sent ... to say to those who were invited, that they should come; for now all things were ready. And they began all at once to make excuse. (St. Luke, c. xiv., vv. 17-18.)

And if I send them away fasting ... they will faint in the way. (St. Mark, c. viii., v. 3.)

My heart is withered; because I forgot to eat my bread. (Ps. ci.)

1. Frequent communion is the most efficacious of all means to unite us to God. "He that eateth my flesh," said our divine Saviour, "abideth in Me and I in him."(6)

2. St. Bernard calls the Holy Eucharist the love of loves. Hence you should desire to receive it frequently in order to be filled with this divine love.
3. St. Francis de Sales says there are two classes of persons who should often receive holy communion; the perfect, to unite themselves more closely to the Source of all perfection, and the imperfect to labor to attain perfection; the strong that they may not become weak, the weak that they may become strong; the sick that they may be cured, and those in health that they may be preserved from sickness. You tell me that your imperfections, your weakness, your littleness make you unworthy to receive communion frequently; and I assure you it is precisely because of these that you ought to receive it frequently in order that He who pos-

sesses all things may give you whatever is wanting to you.

*The following words on this subject will not perhaps be considered by others as giving much additional value to the authority of the saintly Bishop of Geneva. They do so, however, in ours, because they are from the lips of a holy religious whose memory will always be dear to us——from a man whose last moments were the occasion of the greatest edification it has ever pleased God to accord us. The Rev. Father Margottet, a Jesuit, died at Nice, April 1st, 1835, shortly after his return from Portugal where he had suffered a most cruel captivity with the courage that faith alone can inspire. During the last months of his life he took great pleasure in conversing with a certain young man who visited him regularly to be instructed and edified by his pious discourse. One day this young man confided to him the confusion he felt in availing himself of his director's permission to receive holy Communion several times a week. This was due especially to the thought that St. Aloysius, whilst a novice of the Society of Jesus, went to Communion on Sundays only. "Come, come, my dear sir," laughingly replied the good Father, "continue your frequent Communions—you need them much more than St. Aloysius did." It is indeed an error to consider holy Communion a reward of virtue, and, in a measure, a guage of perfection, whereas it is above all a means to attain perfection, and the one pre-existing virtue required in order to employ this means is the desire to profit by it. Our divine Lord did not say: Venite ad me qui perfecti estis—Come to Me all ye who are perfect: He said: Venite ad me qui laboratis et onerati estis(7)—Come to me all ye who labor and are burdened. (Read Chapters XX. and XXI., Part II., of the Introduction to a Devout Life; and Chapters X. and XVI. Book IV. of The Imitation.)

The spirit of the Church has at all times been the same in regard to this important subject. Fénelon says in his letter on frequent Communion that St. Chrysostom admits of no medium between the state of those who are in mortal sin and that of the faithful who are in a state of grace and communicate every day. In vain certain Christians, believing themselves purified and just, do no penance as sinners and nevertheless abstain from Communion, because, they say, they are not perfect enough to receive it. This intermediate state is not only most dangerous for one who wilfully remains in it, but is also injurious to the Blessed Sacrament. Far from doing honor to the Holy Eucharist by depriving ourselves of it, we offend our divine Lord when we decline to partake of the Banquet to which He invites us. In a word, according to this early Father of the Church, we ought either to communicate with those who are in a state of grace, or to do penance that we may be united to them as soon as possible.

We will quote the Saint's own words: "Many of the faithful are weak and languishing, many among them sleep. And how, you say, does this happen since we receive the Blessed Sacrament but once a year? That is precisely the cause of all the trouble! For you imagine that merit consists not so much in purity of conscience as in the length of time intervening between your Communions. You consider no higher mark of respect and honor can be paid to this Sacrament than not to approach the Holy Table often.... Temerity does not consist in approaching the Altar frequently, but in approaching it unworthily were this but once in an entire life time.... Why then regulate the number of Communions by the law of time, instead of by purity of conscience, which should alone indicate how many times to receive? This divine Mystery is nothing more at Easter than at all other seasons during which it is celebrated continually. It is ever the same, that is to say, ever the same gift of the Holy Ghost. Easter continues throughout the year. You who are initiated will understand perfectly what I say. Be it Saturday, or Sunday, or the feasts of the martyrs, it is always the same Victim, the same Sacrifice." "It was not the will of our divine Lord that His Sacrifice should be restricted by the observance of time."

Other Fathers of the Church speak in the same way of Holy Communion:

"If it is daily bread," says Saint Ambrose, "why do you partake of it but once a year?... Receive it every day in order that every day you may benefit by it. Live in such a manner that you may deserve to receive it every day, for he who does not deserve to receive it every day will not deserve to receive it at the end of the year.... Do you not know that every time the Holy Sacrifice is offered, the death, resurrection and ascension of our Lord are renewed to the atonement of sin? And yet you will not partake daily of this Bread of Life! When one has received a wound does he not seek a remedy? Sin which holds us captive is our wound: our remedy is in this ever adorable Sacrament."

In order that it may be plainly proved that the faithful of the present day have no reason to act differently in this respect from those of the primitive Church, let us see how this ancient discipline has been confirmed in later times by the Council of Trent:

"Christians should believe in this Sacrament and reverence it with such a firm faith, with so much fervor and piety, that they may often receive this Super-substantial Bread; that it may be, in truth, the life of their soul and the perpetual health of their spirit, and that the strength they derive therefrom may enable them to pass from the temptations of this earthly pilgrimage to the repose of their heavenly father-land.... The Council would have the faithful receive Communion each time they assist at Mass, not only spiritually, but sacramentally, that they may derive more abundant fruit from the Holy Sacrifice."*

4. The evening before your Communion devote some little time to recollection in order to ponder the inestimable gift that God is about to bestow upon you, and endeavor also to excite in your soul the desire and the hope of finding therein your delight.

5. Do not conclude that you derive no benefit from Holy Communion because you find no perceptible increase in your virtues. Consider that it at least serves to keep you in a state of grace. You give nourishment to your body every day but you do not pretend to say that it daily gains in strength. Does food appear useless to you on that account? Certainly not; for, though it fail to augment strength, it preserves it by repairing the constant waste. Now, this is precisely the case with the divine Food of our souls.

*Observe, moreover, that there is no real increase in virtue without a corresponding growth in humility. Consequently the more virtuous you are the less so you will esteem yourself; the worthier you are to approach your God, the more profoundly will you feel your unworthiness. For man, no matter to what degree of virtue he attain, cannot be otherwise than weak and sinful here below, and he realizes his baseness more and more distinctly in proportion to his advancement in grace and in light.

Fénelon speaks as follows on the same subject: "Hitherto

you lacked the light to discover in your soul many movements of our malicious and depraved nature, which now begin to reveal themselves to you. In proportion as light increases we find ourselves more corrupt than we supposed: but we should be neither surprised nor discouraged, for it is not that we are in reality worse than we were,—on the contrary we are better,—but because whilst our sinfulness decreases the light which shows it to us increases."*

6. Do not fear that you are ill-prepared for Holy Communion and abuse the Sacrament because in receiving it you are cold, indifferent, and devoid of feeling. This is a trial sent or permitted by God to test your faith and to advance you in merit. All that has been said in regard to dryness in prayer might be repeated here. Try to have an abiding desire to feel for the Blessed Eucharist as ardent transports of love as were ever experienced by the saints. A desire is equivalent before God to the thing desired, as I have already quoted for you from Saint Gregory the Great; therefore you should be satisfied with this when you can attain nothing higher. Everything over and above this is grace, not merit.

7. If you dare not receive Holy Communion often because you are not worthy, then you must never receive it, for you will never be worthy. What creature could be worthy to receive a God? Nay more, to follow out this principle We should have to abandon the practice of visiting churches and of speaking to God in prayer; for a miserable, sin-stained human being is unfit to enter the House of the Lord or to converse with Him.

*"How many scrupulous Christians do we not see languishing for want of this divine Food! They consume themselves with subtle speculations and sterile efforts, they fear, they

51

tremble, they doubt, and they vainly seek for a certainty that cannot be found in this life. Sweetness, unction, are not for them. They wish to live for God without living by him. They are dry, feeble, exhausted: they are close to the Fountain of Living Water and yet allow themselves to die of thirst. They desire to fulfil all exteriorly, yet do not dare to nourish themselves interiorly: they wish to carry the burden of the law without imbibing its spirit and its consolation from prayer and frequent Communion!"—Fénelon.*

8. In regard to Holy Communion, therefore, do not confine yourself to a consideration of your own unworthiness, but temper this with the thought of God's mercy. The guests at the symbolic marriage-feast,—a figure of the Holy Eucharist,—were not the great and the rich, but the poor, the blind, the lame. Whosoever is clothed in the nuptial garment, that is to say, whosoever is in a state of grace, is welcome to this banquet.

9. St. Francis de Sales says that when we cannot go to Holy Communion without giving annoyance to others, or without failing against duties of charity, justice or order, we should be satisfied with spiritual Communion. "Believe me," he adds, "this mortification, this deprivation, will be extremely pleasing to God and will advance you greatly in His love. One must sometimes take a step backward in order to leap the better." It was not by frequent Communion that the holy anchorites sanctified themselves, but by the exact observance of the duties of their calling. Saint Paul the Hermit received Holy Communion but twice during his long, penitential life, nevertheless he was precious in the sight of God. A propos of this subject Saint Francis de Sales gives us this admirable advice: "In proportion as you are hindered from doing the good you desire, do all the more ardently the good

that you do not desire. You do not like to make such or such an act of resignation, you would prefer to make some other; but offer the one you do not like, for it will be of far greater value." Saint John the Baptist was more intimately united in spirit with our Lord than even the Apostles themselves: yet he never became one of His followers owing to the fact that his vocation required this sacrifice on his part and called him elsewhere. This is the greatest act of spiritual mortification recorded in the lives of the saints.

"I have often admired the extreme resignation of Saint John the Baptist, who remained so long in the desert, quite near to our Lord, without going to see, hear and follow Him. And after baptizing Jesus, how could he have allowed Him to depart without uniting himself to Him with his bodily presence, as he was already so united to Him by the ties of affection! Ah! the divine Precursor knew that in his case the Master was best served by deprivation of His actual presence. Well, my dear daughter, it will be the same with you in regard to Holy Communion. I mean that for the present God will be pleased if in accordance to the wish of the superiors whom He has placed over you, you endure the privation of His actual presence. It will be a great consolation to me to know that this advice does not disquiet your heart. Rest assured that this resignation, this renunciation will be exceedingly beneficial to you."—St. Francis de Sales.

11. Never refrain from receiving the Holy Eucharist because you happen to be beset by temptations; this would be to capitulate to your enemy without offering any resistance. The more combats you have to sustain, the greater the necessity of providing yourself with the means of defence, and these are to be found in the Blessed Sacrament. Go courageously then and renew your strength with the Food of the strong

and victory shall be yours.

12. Be careful not to frequent the Holy Table because such and such a person does so: an imitation common for the most part to women's vanity and jealousy, says Saint Francis de Sales. It is through love that our divine Saviour gives Himself to us in the Blessed Sacrament: love alone should lead us to receive it.

13. Holy Communion should not be partaken of with the same frequency by all the faithful. All, indeed, must have the same object in view, that is union with God, but the same means to attain that object are not proper for every one. It is only by obedience to the advice of a spiritual director that each person can know what is suitable for him, as that which would be too little for one might be too much for another.

VII.
SUNDAYS AND HOLYDAYS.

The sabbath was made for man, and not man for the sabbath. (St. Mark, c. II., v: 27.)

1. Every day of our life should be employed in glorifying God, but there are certain days He has particularly appointed whereon to receive from us a more special exterior worship. These are Sundays and holydays.

2. It is therefore obligatory upon us to sanctify such days. The ordinary means of fulfilling this duty are, principally, works of charity, the Holy Sacrifice of the Mass, the Sacraments, sermons, religious instructions, and spiritual reading.

3. Nevertheless, we should avoid over-fatiguing the mind and wearying the body by too many exercises of devotion. Excess even in holy things is wrong, as virtue ends where excess begins. All that was said on this subject in the chapter on Prayer is equally applicable here.

4. Moreover it is well to know that a friendly visit, a walk, a lawful diversion, all of which can be referred to God, serve also for the sanctification of Sundays and holydays, when undertaken with a view to please Him. The same may be said of such daily occupations as are required of man by his bodily needs.

*"How often we are mistaken in our point of view! I tell you once again it is not the outward aspect of actions that we must look at, but their interior spirit, that is to say, whether or not they are according to the will of God. By no means regard the nature of the things you do, but rather the honor

that accrues to them, worthless as they are in themselves, from the fact that God wishes them, that they are in the order of his providence and disposed by His infinite wisdom. In a word, if they are pleasing to God, and recognized as being so, to whom should they be displeasing?"—Saint Francis de Sales.*

5. These things are said for the instruction of those who are eager and anxious on Sundays and holydays of obligation to heap devotion upon devotion and who make a crime of everything that is not an exterior act of piety. They apply themselves, it seems, to the material observance of the sabbath, following the superstitious custom of the Pharisees, instead of peacefully sanctifying the Lord's day with that sweet and holy liberty of spirit which our divine Saviour teaches in the Gospel. Too much dissipation and over long prayers are two extremes each of which it is equally necessary to avoid.

6. Should it happen that you are obliged to travel on Sunday or to attend to some unforseen business, do not be disquieted about the impossibility of fulfilling your customary devout exercises. Replace these with pious ejaculations, which, as I have already said, can in case of necessity supply for the omission of all other prayers.

7. Remark, in conclusion, that to assist at a low Mass suffices strictly speaking for the sanctification of the Sunday or holyday. Even this may be omitted by those persons whom duty obliges to attend the sick, to mind the house, or to take care of young children; for these being works of justice and charity and good in themselves, may, when performed with a pure intention and accompanied by ejaculatory prayers, equal and even surpass in value all exterior practices of devotion.

I do not speak at all of the sick, for by their sufferings they can sanctify every day and make each one equal to the greatest festival.

"Worldly notions are forever blending with our thoughts and throwing them out of perspective. In the house of an earthly prince it is not so honorable to be a scullion in the kitchen as to be a gentleman-in-waiting. But it is different in the house of God, where those in the humblest positions are oft-times the most worthy; for although they labor and drudge it is done for the love of God and in fulfilment of His divine will; and the true value of our actions is fixed by this divine will and not by their exterior character. Therefore he who truly loves God's will in the accomplishment of his duties, does not allow his affections to become engaged in any of his spiritual exercises; and so, if sickness or accident interfere with them he experiences no regret. I do not say indeed that he does not love his devotions, but that he is not attached to them."—Saint Francis de Sales.

"If you have a sincere regard for the virtues of obedience and submission, I wish that, should justice or charity demand it, you would forego your pious exercises, which would be a sort of obedience, and that this omission should be supplied by love. I told you on another occasion: the less we live according to our own liking, and the less option we have in our actions, the more goodness and solidity will there be in our devotion. It is right and proper sometimes to leave our Lord in order to oblige others for love of Him."—Saint Francis de Sales.

VIII.
SPIRITUAL READING.

Blessed is the man whom Thou shalt instruct, O Lord, and shalt teach him out of Thy Law. (Ps. XCIII, v. 12.)

All scripture divinely inspired, is profitable to teach, to reprove, to correct, to instruct in justice. (S. P. Timoth., Ep. II, iii, 16.)

1. Spiritual reading is to the soul what food is to the body. Be careful, therefore, to select such books as will furnish your soul with the best nourishment. I would recommend you to become familiar especially with the works of Saint Francis de Sales.

2. When the choice of reading matter is made by the advice of a spiritual director the teaching it contains should be looked upon as coming from the mouth of God.

3. Do not affect those lives of the Saints in which the supernatural and marvellous predominate. The devout imagination becomes inflamed by such reading and is imbued with vain and useless desires: it leads some to aspire to the revelations of Saint Bridget or the raptures of Saint Joseph of Cupertino, others to imitate the mortifications of the Stylites; and thus by losing time in desiring extraordinary graces, they neglect, to their great detriment, ordinary duties and real obligations. Take great care, then, not to allow yourself to be absorbed in those wonderful characteristics of the saints which we should be content to admire; give preference rather to their simple and interior virtues, for these alone are imitable for us.

"We ought not to wish for extraordinary things, as, for example, that God would take away our heart, as He did with Saint Catherine of Sienna's, and give us His in return. But we should desire that our poor hearts no longer live save in subjection to the Heart of our loving Saviour, and this will be the best way of imitating Saint Catherine, for we shall thus become meek, humble and charitable.... True holiness consists in love of God, and not in foolish imaginations and dreamings that nourish self-love whilst they undermine obedience and humility. The desire to have ecstacies and visions is a deception. Let us turn rather to the practice of true meekness and submissiveness, of self-renunciation and docility, of ready compliance with the wishes of others. Thus we shall emulate the saints in what is more real and more admirable for us than ecstacies."—St. Francis de Sales.

4. Use still greater precautions in regard to ascetical works. Many of these are carelessly written, confound precepts with counsels, badly define the virtues by not showing the limits beyond which they become extravagances, and entertain the reader with trifling and purely exterior practices that are more apt to flatter self-love than to reform the heart.

5. It has been remarked very justly by a learned theologian that the ignorance and indiscreet zeal of certain writers of ascetical books have furnished the heretics of later times with arms to attack our holy religion and to turn it into ridicule.

6. A judicious author expresses himself thus on the same subject: "In order to write on spiritual matters it is not enough to have great piety,—great learning is also necessary. A man actuated by the best motives in the world may yet have strange delusions, and feed his imagination with devout extravagances." An author should be equally well versed in

theory and experienced in practice, otherwise he will err either in regard to principles or to their application. There is a well known saying generally attributed to Saint Thomas: "If a man be good and holy let him pray for us; if he be learned too, then let him teach us." It is essential, in matters of religion especially, to give none but true and precise ideas, or else they will do more harm than good. Doctrines that are not exact create scruples in weak souls and invite the criticisms of intelligent Christians, whilst they excite the railleries of free-thinkers and furnish arguments to unbelievers.

7. Almost every day we find ascetical works published which contain many inaccuracies of the kind described. Exercise great care, therefore, in the selection of this kind of reading or you may injure your soul instead of sanctifying it. The safest course is to consult your director on the subject.

PART SECOND.
INTERIOR LIFE.

IX.
HOPE.

Casting all your solicitude upon Him for He hath care of you. (St. Petr., Ep. I., c. V., v. 7.)

Let Thy mercy descend upon us according to the trust we have placed in Thee. (Cant. Saint Ambrose.)

1. "Blessed is the man who hopes in the Lord," says the Holy Spirit. The weakness of our souls is often attributable to lukewarmness in regard to the Christian virtue of hope.

2. Hold fast to this great truth: he who hopes for nothing will obtain nothing; he who hopes for little will obtain little; he who hopes for all things will obtain all things.

3. The mercy of God is infinitely greater than all the sins of the world. We should not, then, confine ourselves to a consideration of our own wretchedness, but rather turn our thoughts to the contemplation of this divine attribute of mercy.

4. "What do you fear?" says Saint Thomas of Villanova: "this Judge whose condemnation you dread is the same Jesus Christ who died upon the Cross in order not to condemn you."

5. Sorrow, not fear, is the sentiment our sins should awaken in us. When Saint Peter said to his divine Master: "Depart from me, O Lord, for I am a sinful man," what did our Sav-

iour reply? "Noli timere,—fear not."(8) Saint Augustine remarks that in the Holy Scriptures we always find hope and love preferred to fear.

6. Our miseries form the throne of the divine mercy, we are told by Saint Francis de Sales, for if in the world there were neither sins to pardon, nor sorrows to soothe, nor maladies of the soul to heal, God would not have to exercise the most beautiful attribute of His divine essence. This was our Lord's reason for saying that He came into the world not for the just but for sinners.(9)

7. Assuredly our faults are displeasing to God, but He does not on their account cease to cherish our souls.

It is unnecessary to observe that this applies only to such faults as are due to the frailty inherent in our nature, and against which an upright will, sustained by divine grace, continually struggles. A perverse will, without which there can be no mortal sin, alienates us from God and renders us hateful in His eyes as long as we are subject to it. At the feast spoken of in the Gospel, the King receives with love the poor, the blind, and the lame who are clothed with the nuptial garment,—that is to say, all those whom a desire to please God maintains in a state of grace notwithstanding their natural defects and frailty: but his rigorous justice displays itself against him who dares to appear there without this garment. This distinction, found everywhere throughout the Gospels, is essential in order to inspire us with a tender confidence when we fall, without diminishing our horror for deliberate sins.

A good mother is afflicted at the natural defects and infirmities of her child, but she loves him none the less, nor does she refuse him her compassion or her aid. Far from it; for the more miserable and suffering and deformed he may be the greater is her tenderness and solicitude for him.

8. We have, says Saint Paul, a good and indulgent High-Priest who knows how to compassionate our weakness, Jesus Christ, who has been pleased to become at once our Brother and our Mediator.(10)

9. Do not forfeit your peace of mind by wondering what destiny awaits you in eternity. Your future lot is in the hands of God, and it is much safer there than if in your own keeping.

10. The immoderate fear of hell, in the opinion of Saint Francis de Sales, can not be cured by arguments, but by submission and humility.

11. Hence it was that Saint Bernard, when tempted by the devil to a sin of despair, retorted: "I have not merited heaven, I know that as well as you do, Satan; but I also know that Jesus Christ, my Saviour, has merited it for me. It was not for Himself that He purchased so many merits,—but for me: He cedes them to me, and it is by Him and in Him that I shall save my soul."

12. Far from allowing yourself to be dejected by fear and doubt, raise your desires rather to great virtues and to the most sublime perfection. God loves courageous souls, Saint Theresa assures us, provided they mistrust their own strength and place all their reliance upon Him. The devil tries to persuade you that it is pride to have exalted aspirations and to wish to imitate the virtues of the saints; but do not permit him to deceive you by this artifice. He will only laugh at you if he succeed in making you fall into weakness

and irresolution.

To aspire to the noblest and highest ends gives firmness and perseverance to the soul. (Read The Imitation, B. III, C. XXX.)

X.
THE PRESENCE OF GOD.

Walk before Me and be perfect. (Genesis, c. XVII, v. 1.)

I have lifted up my eyes to the mountains, from whence help shall come to me. (Psalm CXX, v. 1.)

1. The constant remembrance of God's presence is a means of perfection that Almighty God Himself prescribed to the Patriarch Abraham. But this practice must be followed gently and without effort or disturbance of mind. The God of love and peace wishes that all we do for Him should be done lovingly and peacefully.

2. Only in heaven shall we be able to think actually and uninterruptedly of God. In this world to do so is an impossibility, for we are at every moment distracted by our occupations, our necessities, our imagination. We but exhaust ourselves by futile efforts if we try to lead before the proper time an existence similar to that of the angels and saints.

3. Frequently the fear comes to you that you have failed to keep yourself in the presence of God, because you have not thought of Him. This is a mistaken idea. You can, without this definite thought, perform all your actions for love of God and in His presence, by virtue of the intention you had in beginning them. Now, to act is better than to think. Though the doctor may not have the invalid in mind while he is preparing the medicine that is to restore him to health, nevertheless it is for him he is working, and he is more useful to his patient in this way than if he contented himself with merely thinking of him. In like manner when you fulfil your domestic or social duties, when you eat or walk, devote yourself to study or to manual labor, though it be without

definitely thinking of God, you are acting for Him, and this ought to suffice to set your mind at rest in regard to the merit of your actions. Saint Paul does not say that we must eat, drink and labor with an actual remembrance of God's presence, but with the habitual intention of glorifying Him and doing His holy will. We fulfil this condition by making an offering each morning to God of all the actions of the day and renewing the act interiorly whenever we can remember to do so.

4. For this purpose, make frequent use of ejaculatory prayers. We have already spoken of them. Accustom yourself to make these pious aspirations naturally and without effort, and let them for the most part be expressive of confidence and love.

5. Should it happen that a considerable space of time elapses without your having thought distinctly of God or raised your heart to Him by any loving ejaculation, do not allow this omission to worry you. The servant has performed his duty and deserves well of his master when he has done his will, even though he may not have been thinking of him the while. Always bear in mind the fact that it is better to work for God than to think of Him. Thought has its highest spiritual value when it results in action: action is meritorious in itself by virtue of the good intention which preceded it.

XI.
HUMILITY.

If I glorify myself, my glory is nothing. (St. John, c. VIII, v. 54.)

For behold I was born in iniquities: and in sins did my mother conceive me. (Psalm L., v. 7.)

1. Few persons have a correct idea of this virtue. It is frequently confused with servility or littleness.

2. To attribute to God what is God's, that is to say everything that is good, and to ourselves what is ours, that is to say, everything that is evil: these are the essential characteristics of true humility.

Hence it would appear at first sight that simple good sense ought to suffice to make men humble. Such would be the case were it not that our faculties have been impaired and vitiated in their very source by pride, that direful and ineffaceable consequence of original sin. The first man, a creature owing his existence directly to God, was bound to dedicate it entirely to Him and to pay continual homage for it is as for all the other gifts he had received. This was a duty of simple justice. The day whereon he asserted a desire to be independent, he caused an utter derangement in the relations of the creature with his Creator. Pride, that tendency to self-sufficiency, to refer to self the use of the faculties received from God—pride, introduced into the soul of the first man by a free act of his will, has attached itself as an indelible stigma to the souls of all his descendants, and has become forevermore a part of their nature. Thence comes this inclination, ever springing up afresh, to be independent, to be something of ourselves, to desire for ourselves esteem, affection and honor, despite the precepts of the divine law, the claims of justice and the warnings of reason; and thus it is that the whole spiritual life is but one long and painful conflict against this vicious propensity. Divine grace though sustaining us in the combat never gives us a complete victory, for the struggle must endure until death,—the closing chastisement of our original degradation and the only one that can obliterate the last traces thereof. (See Imitation, B. III., Ch. XIII.—XXII.)

3. As God drew from nothingness everything that exists, in like manner does He wish to lay the foundations of our spiritual perfection upon the knowledge of our nothingness. Saint Bonaventure used to say: Provided God be all, what matters it that I am nothing!

4. When a Christian who is truly humble commits a fault he repents but is not disquieted, because he is not surprised that what is naught but misery, weakness and corruption, should be miserable, weak and corrupt. He thanks God on the contrary that his fall has not been more serious. Thus Saint Catherine of Genoa, whenever she found she had been guilty of some imperfection, would calmly exclaim: Another weed from my garden! This peaceful contemplation of our sinfulness was considered very important by Saint Francis de Sales also, for he says: "Let us learn to bear with our imperfections if we wish to attain perfection, for this practice nourishes the virtue of humility."

5. Some persons have the erroneous idea that in order to be humble they must not recognize in themselves any virtue or talent whatsoever. The reverse is the case according to Saint Thomas, for he says it is necessary to realize the gifts we

have received that we may return thanks for them to Him from whom we hold them. To ignore them is to fail in gratitude towards God, and to neglect the object for which He gave them to us. All that we have to do is to avoid the folly of taking glory to ourselves because of them. Mules, asses and donkeys may be laden with gold and perfumes and yet be none the less dull and stupid animals. The graces we have received, far from giving us any personal claims, only serve to increase our debt to Him who is their source and their donor.

6. Praise is naturally more pleasing to us than censure. There is nothing sinful in this preference, for it springs from an instinct of our human nature of which we cannot entirely divest ourselves. Only the praise must be always referred to Him to whom it is due, that is to say, to God; for they are His gifts that are praised in us as we are but their bearers and custodians and shall one day have to render Him an account for them in accordance with their value.

7. The soul that is most humble will also have the greatest courage and the most generous confidence in God; the more it distrusts itself, the more it will trust in Him on whom it relies for all its strength, saying with Saint Paul: I can do all things in Him who strengtheneth me.(11) Saint Thomas clearly proves that true Christian humility, far from debasing the soul, is the principle of everything that is really noble and generous. He who refuses the work to which God calls him because of the honor and éclat that accompany it, is not humble but mistrustful and pusillanimous. We shall find in obedience light to show us with certainty that to which we are called and to preserve us from the illusions of self-love and of our natural inclinations.

"We should be actuated by a generous and noble humility, a humility that does nothing in order to be praised and omits nothing that ought to be done through fear of being praised."—Saint Francis de Sales.

8. It is even good and sometimes necessary to make known the gifts we have received from God and the good works of which divine grace has made us the instruments, when this manifestation can conduce to the glory of His name, the welfare of the Church, or the edification of the faithful. It was for this threefold object that Saint Paul spoke of his apostolic labors and supernatural revelations.

XII.
RESIGNATION.

Yea, Father: because so it has pleased Thee. (St. Luke, c. X., v. 21.)

O my Father, if it be possible, let this chalice pass from me. Nevertheless not as I will, but as Thou wilt. (St. Matthew, c. XXVI., v. 39.)

1. We should recognize and adore the will of God in everything that happens to us. The malice of men, nay of the devil himself, can cause nothing to befall us except what is permitted by God. Our divine Lord has declared that not a hair of our heads can fall unless by the will of our Heavenly Father.(12)

2. Therefore in every condition painful to nature, whether you are afflicted by sickness, assailed by temptations, or tortured by the injustice of men, consider the divine will and say to God with a loving and submissive heart: Fiat voluntas tua—Thy will be done: O my Saviour, do with me what Thou willest, as Thou willest, and when Thou willest.

3. By this means we render supportable the severest pain and the most trying circumstances. "Do you not feel the infinite sweetness contained in that one sentence, the will of God?" asks Saint Mary Magdalen de Pazzi. Like unto the wood shown to Moses, that drew from the water all its bitterness, it sweetens whatever is bitter in our lives.

4. Without this practice, so comfortable to faith, and without the light and strength that result from it, the pains and afflictions of life would become unbearable. This is what

Saint Philip de Neri meant when he said: It rests with man to place himself even in this life either in heaven or in hell: he who suffers tribulations with patience enjoys celestial peace in advance; he who does not do so has a foretaste of the torments of hell.

5. Not only is it God who sends or permits our troubles, but He does so for the good of our souls and for our spiritual progress. Do not, then, make a matter of complaint that which should be a motive for gratitude.

6. Saint Francis de Sales says that the cross is the royal door to the temple of sanctity, and the only one by which we can enter it. One moment spent upon the cross is therefore more conducive to our spiritual advancement than the anticipated enjoyment of all the delights of heaven. The happiness of those who have reached their destination consists in the possession of God: to suffer for the love of Him is the only true happiness which those still on the way can expect to attain. Our Lord declared that those who mourn during this exile are blessed, for they shall be consoled eternally in their celestial fatherland.(13)

7. Notice that I say, to suffer for the love of God, for, as Saint Augustine remarks, no person can love suffering in itself. That is contrary to nature, and moreover, there would no longer be any suffering if we could accept it with natural relish. But a resigned soul loves to suffer, that is she loves the virtue of patience and ardently desires the merits that result from the practice of it. A calm and submissive longing to be delivered from our cross if such be the will of God, is not inconsistent with the most perfect resignation. This desire is a natural instinct which supernatural grace regulates, moderates, and teaches us to control, but which it never entirely

destroys. Our divine Saviour Himself, to show that He was truly man, was pleased to feel it as we do, and prayed that the chalice of His Passion might be spared Him. Hence you are not required to be stolidly indifferent or to arm yourself with the stern insensibility of the Stoics; that would not be either resignation, or humility, or any virtue whatsoever. The essential thing is to suffer with Christian patience and generous resignation everything that is naturally displeasing to us. This is what both reason and faith prescribe.

*The Redeemer of the World seems to wish to show us in His Agony the degree of perfection which the weakness of human nature can attain amidst the anguish of sorrow. In the inferior portion of the soul where the faculty of feeling resides, instinctive repugnance to suffering, humble prayer for relief if it please God to accord it; and in the superior portion of the soul where the will resides, entire resignation if this consolation be denied. A desire for more than this, unless called to it by a special grace, would be foolish pride, as we should thus attempt to change the conditions of our nature, whereas our duty is to accept them in order to combat them and to suffer in so doing. (See Imitation, B. III., Ch. XVIII-XIX.)

In the following terms Saint Francis de Sales proposes to us this same example of our Saviour's resignation during His agony: "Consider the great dereliction our Divine Master suffered in the Garden of Olives. See how this beloved Son, having asked for consolation from His loving Father and knowing that it was not His will to grant it, thinks no more about it, no longer craves or looks for it, but, as though He had never sought it, valiantly and courageously completes the work of our redemption. Let it be the same with you. If your Heavenly Father sees fit to deny you the consolation you have prayed for, dismiss it from your mind and animate your courage to fulfil your work upon the cross as if you were never to descend from it nor should ever again see the atmosphere of your life pure and serene." (Read The Imitation. B. III., Chapters XI and XV.)

The same Saint also gives us some sublime lessons in resignation applied to the trials and temptations that beset the spiritual life. He draws them from this great and simple thought that serves as foundation for the Exercises of Saint Ignatius, namely, that salvation being the sole object of our existence, and all the attendant circumstances of life but means for attaining it, nothing has any absolute value; and that the only way of forming a true estimate of things is to consider in how far they are calculated to advance or retard the end in view. Accordingly, what difference does it make if we attain this end by riches or poverty, health or sickness, spiritual consolation or aridity, by the esteem or contempt of our fellow-men? So say faith and reason; but human nature revolts against this indifference, as it is well it should, else how could we acquire merit? Hence there is a conflict on this point between the flesh and the spirit, and it is this conflict that for a Christian is called life. (On this subject read The Imitation, B. II., Ch. XI.; and B. III., Ch. XVIII., XIX., XXXVII., XLIX., L. and the prayer at the end of Ch. XXVII.)

"Would to God," he says elsewhere, speaking on the same subject, "that we did not concern ourselves so much about the road whereon we journey, but rather would keep our eyes fixed on our Guide and upon that blessed country whither He is conducting us. What should it matter to us if it be through deserts or pleasant fields that we walk, provided God be with us and we be advancing towards heaven?... In short, for the honor of God, acquiesce perfectly in his divine will, and do not suppose that you can serve him better in any other way; for no one ever serves him well who does not serve him as he wishes. Now he wishes that you serve him without relish, without feeling, nay, with repugnance and perturbation of spirit. This service does not afford you any satisfaction, it is true, but it pleases him; it is not to your taste, but it is to his.... Mortify yourself then cheerfully, and in proportion as you are prevented from doing the good you desire, do all the more ardently that which you do not desire. You do not wish to be resigned in this case, but you will be so in some other: resignation in the first instance will be of much greater value to you.... In fine, let us be what God wishes, since we are entirely devoted to him, and would not wish to be anything contrary to his will; for were we the most exalted creatures under heaven, of what use would it be to us, if we were not in accord with the will of God?..."

And again: "You should resign yourself perfectly into the hands of God. When you have done your best towards carrying out your design (of becoming a religious) he will be pleased to accept everything you do, even though it be something less good. You cannot please God better than by sacrificing to him your will, and remaining in tranquillity, humility and devotion, entirely reconciled and submissive to his divine will and good pleasure. You will be able to recognize these plainly enough when you find that notwithstanding all your efforts it is impossible for you to gratify your wishes.

For God in his infinite goodness sometimes sees fit to test our courage and love by depriving us of the things which it seems to us would be advantageous to our souls; and if he finds us very earnest in their pursuit, yet humble, tranquil and resigned to do without them if he wishes us to, he will give us more blessings than we should have had in the possession of what we craved. God loves those who at all times and in all circumstances can say to him simply and heartily: Thy will be done."*

XIII.
SCRUPLES.

Having therefore such hope, we use much confidence. (St. Paul, II. Cor., c. III., v. 12.)

Fear is not in charity: but perfect charity casteth out fear, because fear hath pain. And he that feareth is not perfect in charity. (St. John, I. Epist., c. IV., v. 18.)

1. There are persons who look upon scrupulosity as a virtue, confounding it with delicacy of conscience, whereas it is, on the contrary, not only a defect but one of a most dangerous character. The devout and learned Gerson says that a scrupulous conscience often does more injury to the soul than one that is too lax and remiss.

2. Scruples warp the judgment, disturb the peace of the soul, beget mistrust of the Sacraments and estrangement from them, and impair the health of body and mind. How many unfortunates have begun by scrupulosity and ended in insanity! How many, more unfortunate still, have begun by scruples and ended in laxity and impiety! Shun then this insidious poison, so deadly in its effects on true piety, and say with Saint Joseph of Cupertino: Away with sadness and scruples; I will not have them in my house.

3. Scrupulosity is an unreasonable fear of sin in matters where there is not even material for sin. But the victim does not call his doubts and fears scruples, for he would not be tormented by them if he believed he could give them that name. He should, however, place implicit reliance in the opinion of his spiritual guide when he tells him they are such and that he must not allow himself to be influenced by them.

4. In all his actions a scrupulous person sees only an uninterrupted series of sins, and in God nothing but vengeance and anger. He ought, therefore, to consider almost exclusively the attribute of the divine Master by which He most delights to manifest Himself, mercy, and to make it the constant subject of his thoughts, meditations and affections.

"We should do everything from love and nothing from constraint. It is more essential to love obedience than to fear disobedience."—Saint Francis de Sales.

5. There is but one remedy for scruples and that is entire and courageous obedience. "It is a secret pride," says Saint Francis de Sales, "that entertains and nourishes scruples, for the scrupulous person adheres to his opinion and inquietude in spite of his director's advice to the contrary. He always persuades himself in justification of his disobedience that some new and unforseen circumstance has occurred to which this advice cannot be applicable." "But submit", adds the Saint, "without other reasoning than this: I should obey, and you will be delivered from this lamentable malady."

6. By sadness and anxiety the children of God do a great injury to their Heavenly Father. They thereby seem to bear witness that there is little happiness to be found in the service of a Master so full of love and mercy, and to give the lie to the words of Him who said: "Come unto Me all you that labor and are heavily burdened and I will refresh you."

*"Woe to that narrow and self-absorbed soul that is always fearful, and because of fear has no time to love and to go generously forward. O my God! I know it is your wish that the heart that loves you should be broad and free! Hence I shall act with confidence like to the child that plays in the arms of its mother; I shall rejoice in the Lord and try

to make others rejoice; I shall pour forth my heart without fear in the assembly of the children of God. I wish for nothing but candor, innocence and joy of the Holy Ghost. Far, far from me, O my God, be that sad and cowardly wisdom which is ever consumed in self, ever holding the balance in hand in order to weigh atoms!... Such lack of simplicity in the soul's dealings with Thee is truly an outrage against Thee: such rigor imputed to Thee is unworthy of Thy paternal heart."—Fénelon.*

XIV.
INTERIOR PEACE.

Martha, Martha, thou art careful, and art troubled about many things. (St. Luke, c. X., v. 41.)

Always active, always at rest. (St. Augustine.)

1. Be on your guard lest your zeal degenerate into anxiety and eagerness. Saint Francis de Sales was a most pronounced enemy of these two defects. They cause us to lose sight of God in our actions and make us very prone to impatience if the slightest obstacle should interfere with our designs. It is only by acting peacefully that we can serve the God of peace in an acceptable manner.

"Do not let us suffer our peace to be disturbed by precipitation in our exterior actions. When our bodies or minds are engaged in any work, we should perform it peacefully and with composure, not prescribing for ourselves a definite time to finish it, nor being too anxious to see it completed."— Scupoli.

2. Martha was engaged in a good work when she prepared a repast for our divine Lord, nevertheless He reproved her because she performed it with anxiety and agitation. This goes to show, says Saint Francis de Sales, that it is not enough to do good, the good must moreover be done well, that is to say, with love and tranquillity. If one turn the spinning-wheel too rapidly it falls and the thread breaks.

3. Whenever we are doing well we are always doing enough and doing it sufficiently fast. Those persons who are restless and impetuous do not accomplish any more and what they

do is done badly.

4. Saint Francis de Sales was never seen in a hurry no matter how varied or numerous might be the demands made upon his time. When on a certain occasion some surprise was expressed at this he said: "You ask me how it is that although others are agitated and flurried I am not likewise uneasy and in haste. What would you? I was not put in this world to cause fresh disturbance: is there not enough of it already without my adding to it by my excitability?"

5. However, do not on the other hand succumb to sloth and indifference. All extremes are to be avoided. Cultivate a tranquil activity and an active tranquillity.

6. In order to acquire tranquillity in action it is necessary to consider carefully what we are capable of accomplishing and never to undertake more than that. It is self-love, ever more anxious to do much than to do well, which urges us on to burden ourselves with great undertakings and to impose upon ourselves numerous obligations. It maintains and nourishes itself on this tension of mind, this restless anxiety which it takes for infallible signs of a superior capacity. Thus Saint Francis de Sales was wont to say: "Our self-love is a great braggart, that wishes to undertake everything and accomplishes nothing."

*"It appears to me that you are over eager and anxious in the pursuit of perfection.... Now I tell you truthfully, as it is said in the Book of Kings,(14) that God is not in the great and strong wind, nor in the earthquake, nor in the fire, but in the gentle movement of an almost imperceptible breeze.... Anxiety and agitation contribute nothing towards success. The desire of success is good, but only if it be not accom-

panied by solicitude. I expressly forbid you to give way to inquietude, for it is the mother of all imperfections.... Peace is necessary in all things and everywhere. If any trouble come to us, either of an interior or exterior nature, we should receive it peacefully: if joy be ours, it should be received peacefully: have we to flee from evil, we should do it peacefully, otherwise we may fall in our flight and thus give our enemy a chance to kill us. Is there a good work to be done? we must do it peacefully, or else we shall commit many faults by our hastiness: and even as regards penance,—that too must be done peacefully: Behold, said the prophet, in peace is my bitterness most bitter."(15)*

XV.
SADNESS.

I rejoiced at the things that were said to me: We shall go into the house of the Lord.... Sing joyfully to God, all the earth: serve ye the Lord with gladness.... Why art thou sad, O my soul, and why dost thou trouble me? (Psalms CXXI., XCIX., XLII.)

And God shall wipe away all tears from their eyes. (Apoc. C. XXI., v. 4.)

1. Sadness, says Saint Francis de Sales, is the worst thing in the World, sin alone excepted.

2. It is a dangerous error to seek recollection in sadness: it is the spirit of God that produces recollection; sadness is the work of the spirit of darkness.

3. Do not forget the rule given by Saint Francis de Sales for the discernment of spirits: any thought that troubles and disquiets us cannot come from the God of peace, who makes his dwelling-place only in peaceful souls.

*"Yes, my daughter, I now tell you in writing what I before said to you in person, always be as happy as you can in well-doing, for it gives a double value to good works to be well done and to be done cheerfully. And when I say, rejoice in well-doing, I do not mean that if you happen to commit some fault you should on that account abandon yourself to sadness. For God's sake, no; for that would be to add defect to defect. But I mean that you should persevere in the wish to do well, that you return to it the moment you realize you have deviated from it, and that by means of this fidelity you

live happily in the Lord.... May God be ever in our heart, my daughter.... Live joyfully and be generous, for this is the will of God, whom we love and to whose service we are consecrated."—Saint Francis de Sales.* (Imitation, B. III., Chap. XLVII.)

4. It is wrong to deny one's self all diversion. The mind becomes fatigued and depressed by remaining always concentrated in itself and thus more easily falls a prey to sadness. Saint Thomas says explicitly that one may incur sin by refusing all innocent amusement. Every excess, no matter what its nature, is contrary to order and consequently to virtue.

5. Recreations and amusements are to the life of the soul what seasoning is to our corporal food. Food that is too highly seasoned quickly becomes injurious and sometimes fatal in its effects; that which is not seasoned at all soon becomes unendurable because of its insipidity and unpalatableness.

6. As to the amount of diversion it is right to take, no absolute measure can be given: the rule is that each person should have as much as is necessary for him. This quantity varies according to the bent of the mind, the nature of the habitual occupations, and the greater or less predisposition to sadness one observes in his disposition.

7. When you find your heart growing sad, divert yourself without a moment's delay; make a visit, enter into conversation with those around you, read some amusing book, take a walk, sing, do something, it matters not what, provided you close the door of your heart against this terrible enemy. As the sound of a trumpet gives the signal for a combat, so sad thoughts apprise the devil that a favorable moment has come

for him to attack us.

XVI.
LIBERTY OF SPIRIT.

Now the Lord is a spirit: and where the spirit of the Lord is, there is liberty. (St. Paul, II. Cor., c. III., v. 17.)

For you have not received the spirit of bondage again in fear; but ye have received the spirit of adoption of sons, whereby we cry: Abba, Father. (St. Paul, Romans, c. VIII., v. 15.)

Love God and do what you will. (Saint Augustine.)

1. Christian liberty of spirit, so earnestly recommended by the saints, consists in not becoming the slave of anything, even though good, unless it be of God's will. Thus our purest inclinations, our holiest habits, our wisest rules of conduct, should yield without murmur or complaint to every manifestation of this divine will, in order that they may never become for us obstacles or impediments to good or the occasion of trouble and disquietude. By this means only can we perform all our actions with cheerful confidence and devout courage.

"I leave you the spirit of liberty; not that liberty which hinders obedience, for such is the liberty of the flesh, but that which excludes scruples and constraint.... We ask of God above all things that his name be hallowed, that His kingdom come, that His will be done on earth as it is in heaven. All this implies the spirit of liberty; for provided God's name be sanctified, that His divine Majesty reign in you, that His will be done, the spirit desires nothing more."(16) (Imitation, B. III., Chap. XXVI.)

2. St. Francis de Sales, speaking on this important subject,

says: "He who possesses the spirit of liberty will on no account allow his affections to be mastered even by his spiritual exercises, and in this way he avoids feeling any regret if they are interfered with by sickness or accident. I do not say that he does not love his devotions but that he is not attached to them."

3. A soul that is attached to meditation, if interrupted, will show chagrin and impatience: a soul that has true liberty will take the interruption in good part and show a gracious countenance to the person who was the cause of it. For it is all one to it whether it serve God by meditating or by bearing with its neighbor. Both duties are God's will, but just at this time patience with others is the more essential.

4. The fruits of this holy liberty of spirit are prompt and tranquil submission and generous confidence. Saint Francis de Sales relates that Saint Ignatius ate flesh meat one day in Holy Week simply because his physician thought it expedient for him to do so on account of a slight illness. A spirit of constraint would have made him allow the doctor to spend three days in persuading him, he adds, and would then very probably have refused to yield. I cite this example for the benefit of timid souls and not for those who seek to elude an obligation by unwarranted dispensations.

*This matter is of such importance and a just medium so difficult to follow in practice, that it seems useful to transcribe the following passage from Saint Francis de Sales in its entirety, with the rules and examples it contains, in order that the proper occasions for the exercise of this virtue and its limitations may be well understood.

"A heart possessed of this spirit of liberty is not attached to consolations, but receives afflictions with all the sweetness that is possible to human nature. I do not say that it does not love and desire consolations, but that its affections are not wedded to them.... It seldom loses its joy, for no privation saddens a heart that is not set upon any one thing. I do not say it never loses it, but if it does so it quickly regains it.

The effects of this virtue are sweetness of temper, gentleness, and forbearance towards everything that is not sin or occasion of sin, forming a disposition gently susceptible to the influences of charity and of every other virtue.

The occasions for exercising this holy freedom are found in all those things that happen contrary to our natural inclinations; for one whose affections are not engaged in his own will does not lose patience when his desires are thwarted.

There are two vices opposed to this liberty of spirit,—instability and constraint, or dissipation and servility. The former is a certain excess of freedom which causes us to change our devout exercises or state of life without reason and without knowing if it be God's will. On the slightest pretext practices, plans and rules are altered and for every trivial obstacle our laudable customs are abandoned. In this way the heart is dissipated and spent and becomes like an orchard open on all sides, the fruit whereof is not for the owner but for the passers-by. Constraint or servility is a certain lack of liberty owing to which the mind is overwhelmed with vexation or anger when we cannot carry out our designs, even though we might be doing something better. For example: I resolve to make a meditation every morning. Now if I have the spirit of instability or dissipation I am apt to defer it until evening for the most insignificant reason,—because I was kept awake by the barking of a dog, or because I have a letter to write, although it be not at all pressing. If on the contrary I have the spirit of constraint or servility I will not give up my meditation even though a sick person has great need of my aid just then, or if I have an important and urgent dispatch to send which should not be deferred; and so on.

It remains for me to give you some examples of true liberty of spirit which will make you understand it better than I can explain it. But, before doing so, it is well that I should say there are two rules which it is necessary to observe in order not to make any mistake on the subject.

The first is that a person must never abandon his pious practices and the common rules of virtue unless it is plainly evident that God wills that he do so. Now this will is manifested in two ways,—through necessity and through charity. I desire to preach this Lent in some little corner of my diocese; however, if I get sick or break my leg I need not give way to regret or inquietude because I cannot do as I intended, for it is evident that it is the will of God that I serve Him by suffering and not by preaching. Or, even if I am not ill or crippled, but an occasion presents itself of going to some other place which if I do not avail myself of the people there may become Huguenots, the will of God is sufficiently manifest to make me amiably change my plans. The second rule is that when it is necessary to make use of this liberty of spirit from motives of charity, care should be taken that it is done without scandal or injustice. For instance: I may know that I should be more useful in some distant place not within my own diocese: I should have no freedom of choice in this matter for my obligations are here and I should give scandal and do an injustice by abandoning my charge.

Thus it is a false idea of the spirit of liberty that would induce married women to keep aloof from their husbands without legitimate reason under pretext of devotion and charity.... This spirit rightly understood never interferes with the duties of one's vocation nor prejudices them in any way. On the contrary, it makes every one contented in his state of life, as each should know it is God's will that he remain in it.

Saint Charles Borromeo was one of the most austere, exact and determined of men; bread was his only food, water his only drink; he was so strict, that during the twenty-four years he was an Archbishop he went into his garden but twice, and visited his brothers only on two occasions and then because they were ill. Yet this austere priest when dining with his Swiss neighbors, which he often did in order to move them to amend their lives, did not hesitate to join them in drinking toasts and healths on every occasion and in doing so to take more than was necessary to quench his thirst. Here is true liberty of spirit exemplified in the most mortified man of his time. An unstable spirit would have gone too far, a spirit of constraint would have thought it was committing a mortal sin, a spirit of liberty would act in this way from a motive of charity.

Saint Spiridion, a bishop of olden times, once gave shelter to a pilgrim who was almost dying of hunger. It was the season of Lent and in a place where nothing was to be had but salt meat. This Spiridion ordered to be cooked and then gave it to the pilgrim. Seeing that the latter, notwithstanding his great need, hesitated to eat it, the Saint, although he did not require it, ate some first in order to remove the poor man's scruples. That was a true spirit of liberty born of charity."— Saint Francis de Sales.*

5. Again, it is this Christian spirit of freedom that excludes

fear and uneasiness in regard to all those things which God has not permitted us to know. It gives us a sweet and tender confidence as to the pardon of our past sins, the present condition of our souls and our eternal destiny. It reminds us continually that although we have deserved hell, our divine Lord has merited heaven for us, and that it would be doing a great injury to His goodness not to hope for pardon for the past, assistance of divine grace for the present, and salvation after death. Finally, it teaches us to drown our remorse for sin in the ocean of the divine mercy.

6. I earnestly exhort you never to make indiscreet vows in the hope of thus increasing the merit of your ordinary works. One can attain the same end by many ways that are easier and less dangerous. Those who are guilty of this imprudence often run the risk of breaking their vows and of thus sinning gravely. And if they avoid this misfortune it is only at the expense of their peace of soul, sacrificed to a craven and unquiet servitude which is totally incompatible with the tranquillity and confidence required in the great work of our spiritual perfection.

7. Many pious persons are too prone to advise obligations of this kind. If they do so to you, humbly excuse yourself by saying that you do not possess the extraordinary virtue requisite in order to fulfil them without disquietude. Saint Francis de Sales disapproved of all the particular vows made by Saint Jane Frances de Chantal and declared them null. I have almost invariably found persons bound by such solemn obligations restless and agitated, and have frequently seen them exposed to the gravest falls.

8. Do not allow yourself to be misled by the example of some of the saints who made vows. Rarely is the desire to

imitate certain extraordinary practices of theirs an inspiration of divine grace: rather is it a temptation from the devil inciting us to pride and temerity. Saint Francis de Sales exclaimed: "Give me the spirit that animated Saint Bernard and I shall do what Saint Bernard did." Let us apply ourselves, I repeat, to the imitation of those simple and solid virtues by which the saints attained sanctity, and be content to admire those supernatural acts that suppose it already acquired.

9. To bind one's self by arbitrary vows without compromising salvation, three things are necessary: 1st. supernatural inspiration urging one to make them; 2d. extraordinary virtue so as never to violate them; 3d. unalterable tranquillity in order to preserve peace of soul in keeping them.

XVII.
CHRISTIAN PERFECTION.

Conduct me, O Lord, in Thy way, and I will walk in Thy truth. (Psalm LXXXV.)

Except the Lord build the house, they labor in vain who build it. (Psalm CXXVI.)

1. A Christian is not obliged to be perfect, but to tend continually towards perfection; that is to say, he must labor unceasingly and with all his strength to increase in virtue. To make no attempt to advance is to go back.

*You see it is a question not of succeeding but of laboring earnestly and sincerely. Success does not depend upon us. God grants that or refuses it or defers it according to what He knows is best for us.

"Let us do three things, my dear daughter, says Saint Francis de Sales: first, have a pure intention to look in all things to the honor and glory of God; second, do the little we can towards this end, according to the advice of our spiritual father; third, leave the care of all the rest to God. Why should he torment himself who has God for the object of his intentions and does all that he can? why should he be anxious? what has he to fear? God is not terrible for those whom He loves; He is satisfied with little for He knows well that we have not much to give."

... "Allow yourself to be governed by God; do not think so much of yourself; make a general and universal resolution to serve God in the best manner you are able and do not waste time in examining and sifting so minutely to find out what that may be. This is simply an impertinence due to the condition of your acute and precise mind which wishes to tyrannize over your will and to control it by fraud and subtlety.... You know that in general God wishes us to serve Him by loving Him above all things and our neighbor as ourselves for love of Him; and in particular, to fulfil the duties of our state of life; that is all. But it must be done in good faith, without deceit or subterfuge, and in the ordinary way of this world, which is not the home of perfection; humanly, too, and according to the limitations of time; to do it in a divine and angelic manner and according to eternity being reserved for a future life. Do not therefore be so anxious to know whether or not you have attained perfection. This should never be; for were we the most perfect creatures on earth we ought not to dwell upon or glory in it but always consider ourselves imperfect. Our self-examination must never be for the purpose of discovering if we are imperfect, for this we should never doubt. Hence it follows that we must not be surprised at seeing ourselves imperfect, since we can never be otherwise in this life; nor on that account give way to despondency, for there is no remedy for it. But, yes; we can correct our faults gently and gradually, for that is the reason they are left in us. We shall be inexcusable if we do not try to amend them, but quite excusable if we are not entirely successful in doing so, for it is not the same with imperfections as with sins."—Saint Francis de Sales.*

2. Now the means to be employed in laboring for perfection and in making progress in virtue do not consist in multiplying prayers, fasts and other religious practices. Some good religious who had fasted three times a week during an entire year, thought that in order to satisfy the obligation of advancing more and more in virtue they ought to fast four times a week the following year. They consulted Saint Fran-

cis de Sales on the subject. He laughingly answered them: "If you fast four times a week this year so as to advance in perfection, you will be obliged for the same reason to fast five times the next year, then six, then seven times; and the number of your fasts being always the guage of the degree of perfection you shall have attained, it will be necessary for you, under pain of advancing no more, thereafter to fast twice a day, then thrice, then four times, and so on." What Saint Francis de Sales said of fasting is just as applicable to all other devout practices.

3. Instead, then, of continually adding to your religious exercises, study to perfect yourself in the practice of those you already perform, doing them with more love and peace of soul, and with greater purity of intention. Should it happen that you are unable to perform all your usual devotions conveniently, omit a portion of them so that the remainder may be done with greater tranquillity. The spirit of perfection, says Saint Bernard, does not consist in doing great things, but in doing common and ordinary things perfectly. Communia facere, sed non communiter.(17)

*"Most people when they wish to reform, pay much more attention to filling their life with certain difficult and extraordinary actions, than to purifying their intention and opposing their natural inclinations in the ordinary duties of their state. In this they often deceive themselves, for it would be much better to make less change in the actions and more in the dispositions of the soul which prompt them. When one is already leading a virtuous and well regulated life it is of far greater consequence, in order to become truly spiritual, to change the interior than the exterior. God is not satisfied with the motions of the lips, the posture of the body, nor with external ceremonies: What he demands is a will no lon-

ger divided between Him and any creature; a will perfectly docile ... that wishes unreservedly whatever He wishes and never under any pretext wishes aught that He does not wish.

This will, perfectly simple and entirely devoted to God, you should bear with you into all the circumstances of your life, and everywhere that divine Providence leads you.... Even mere amusements may be transformed into good works, if you enter into them only through a kindly motive and to conform to the order of God. Happy indeed the heart of her for whom God opens this way of holy simplicity! She walks therein like a little child holding its mother's hand and allowing her to lead it without any concern as to whither it is going. Content to be free, she is ready to speak or to be silent; when she cannot say edifying things she says common-place things with an equally good grace; she amuses herself by making what Saint Francis de Sales calls joyeusetés, playful little jests, with which she diverts others as well as herself. You will tell me perhaps that you would prefer to be occupied with something more serious and solid. But God would not prefer it for you, seeing that He chooses what you would not choose, and you know His taste is better than yours: you would find more consolation in solid things for which He has given you a relish, and it is this consolation of which He wishes to deprive you, it is this relish which He wishes to mortify in you, although it may be good and salutary. The very virtues, as they are practised by us, need to be purified by the contradictions that God makes them suffer in order to detach them the better from all self will. When piety is founded on the fundamental principle of God's holy will, without consulting our own taste, or temperament or the sallies of an excessive zeal, oh! how simple, sweet, amiable, discreet and reliable it is in all its movements! A pious person lives much as others do, quite unaffectedly and without apparent austerity, in a sociable and genial way; but with a constant subjection to every duty, an unrelenting renunciation of everything that does not enter into God's designs in her regard, and, finally, with a clear view of God to whom she sacrifices all the irregular inclinations of nature. This indeed is the adoration in spirit and in truth desired by Jesus Christ, our Lord, and His eternal Father. Without it all the rest is but a religion of ceremonial, and rather the shadow than the reality of Christianity."—Fénelon.*

4. Apply yourself in a particular manner to become perfect in the fulfilment of the duties of your state of life; for on this all perfection and sanctity are grounded. When God created the world He commanded the plants to produce fruit, but each one according to its kind: juxta genus suum.(18) In like manner our souls are all obliged to produce fruits of holiness, but each according to its kind; that is to say, according to the position in which God has placed us. Elias in the desert and David on the throne had not to become holy by a like process; and Joshua amidst the tumult of arms would have sought in vain to sanctify himself by the same means as Samuel in the peaceful retreat of the Temple. This instruction is addressed to those who being placed in the world would wish to practise there the virtues of the cloister, or whilst residing in palaces would attempt to lead the life of the solitaries of the desert. They bear fruits which are excellent in themselves, no doubt, but not according to their kind, juxta genus suum, and hence they do not fulfil the will of God.

5. Perfection has but one aim and it is the same for all,—to wit, the love of God; but there are divers ways of attaining it. Among the saints themselves we find most striking differences. Saint Benedict was never seen to laugh, whereas

Saint Francis de Sales laughed frequently and was always animated, bright and cheerful. Saint Hilarion considered it an act of sensuality to change his habit, whilst, on the other hand, Saint Catherine of Sienna was extremely particular about bodily cleanliness which she looked upon as a symbol of purity of soul. If you consult Saint Jerome you hear only of fear of the terrible judgments of God: read Saint Augustine and you will find only the language of confidence and love. The minds, dispositions and characters of men are as varied as their physiognomies; grace perfects them little by little but does not change their nature. Hence in our endeavors to imitate the ways of such or such a saint for whom we feel a particular attraction, we should not condemn those of the others, but say with the Psalmist: Omnis spiritus laudet Dominum.(19) Consult your director as to whom and what may be most suitable for your imitation.

6. Never be afraid that you are not following the way of perfection because you still have defects and commit many faults. This was true of the greatest saints, for Saint Augustine declares that all of them could exclaim with the Apostle Saint John: "If we claim to be without sin, we deceive ourselves and the truth is not in us." "He who came into the world with sin," says Saint Gregory the Great, "cannot live there without sin."

* "Act like the little child who, when it feels that its mother is holding it by the sleeve, runs about quite boldly and without being surprised at all the little falls it gets. Thus, as long as you find that God is holding you by the good will and the resolution He has given you to serve Him, go on bravely and do not be astonished that you stumble and fall occasionally. There is no need to be troubled about it, provided that at certain intervals you cast yourself into your Father's arms

and embrace Him with the kiss of charity. Go on your way, then, cheerfully and heartily, doing the best you can; and if it cannot always be cheerfully, let it at least be always courageously and faithfully." —Saint Francis de Sales.*

7. But we must bear in mind the vast difference that exists between the love of sin and sin committed inadvertently or from weakness. (See Confession, § 14.) Affection for sin is the sole obstacle to perfection. Thus the most learned Fathers of the Church make a distinction between two kinds of tepidity: that which can be avoided and that which cannot be avoided. The former condition is that of a soul that retains an attachment for certain sins; the other, that of one falling into sin through frailty and from being taken unawares, which has been the case even with the greatest saints.

8. Therefore in place of troubling yourself about these accidental falls, inseparable from human nature, make them turn to your spiritual advantage by causing them to increase your humility. It often happens, says Saint Gregory the Great, that God allows great defects to remain in some souls at the beginning of their spiritual life that by means of them they may grow in self-knowledge and learn to place their entire confidence in Him. Saint Augustine tells us that God in his infinite wisdom has been better pleased to bring forth good out of evil than to hinder the evil itself. Thus when you learn to draw fruits of humility from your faults, you correspond to the sublime designs of God's unspeakable providence.

9. Should you happen to fear that you are not walking in the true way of perfection, consult your director and place implicit reliance upon the answer he gives you. Who is the saint that has not had to suffer because of a like doubt? But they were all reassured by the consideration of God's infinite

goodness and by obedience to their spiritual father.

*Some persons, although conscious of a sincere desire to serve God, nevertheless are disposed to feel alarmed about their spiritual condition, at the remembrance of all they have heard and read in regard to false consciences, self-illusion and the deceptive security of those who are following a wrong path. There are two ways of forming a false conscience: first, by choosing among our duties those for which we feel most attraction and natural tendency, and then, in order to give ourselves up to them more than is necessary, to persuade ourselves we can neglect the others. Thus a person with a preference for exterior acts of religion will spend all day praying or attending sermons and offices of the Church and considers herself very devout, although she may have been neglecting her temporal duties. Another, being differently disposed, will apply herself exclusively to the duties of her state of life, sacrificing to them without regret those of religion, quite convinced that one who is faithful in all the domestic relations, and gives to every one his due, cannot possibly be otherwise than pleasing to God. The second way of making a false conscience consists in giving the preference in our esteem and practice to those among the Christian virtues which find their analogies in our natural dispositions, for there is not one of the virtues that has not its correlative amongst the various qualities of the human character. Persons of a gentle and placid disposition will affect meekness, the practice of which will be very easy for them and require no effort; and imagining they exercise a christian virtue when in reality they only follow a natural bent, they are liable to fall into a culpable weakness. Those who, on the contrary, have an exact and rigid mind will esteem justice and order above all else, making small account of meekness and charity; and thus justifying themselves falsely by their natural temperament, they follow the tendency of the flesh whilst believing they obey the spirit, and may easily become addicted to excessive severity.

It is evident, therefore, that the first rule to be observed in order to avoid these dangerous illusions and to walk securely in the way of perfection, is to apply ourselves in a special manner to the practice of those duties for which we feel least innate attraction, and always to mistrust our natural virtues however good they may appear. Then there is one consideration that should serve to reassure all Christians who are in earnest about their salvation; whilst they act in good faith and deal frankly and sincerely with their confessor, it is impossible for them to become the victim of a false conscience.

In the following passage Saint Francis de Sales recommends us to watch carefully over our natural tendencies and to substitute for them as much as possible the inspirations of grace, which he calls living according to the spirit:

"To live according to the spirit, my beloved daughter, is to think, speak and act according to the virtues that are of the spirit, and not according to the senses and feelings which are of the flesh. These latter we should make serve us, but we must hold them in subjection and not allow them to control us; whereas with the spiritual virtues it is just the reverse; we should serve them and bring everything else under subjection to them.... See, my daughter, human nature wishes to have a share in everything that goes on, and loves itself so dearly that it considers nothing of any account unless it be mixed up in it. The spirit, on the contrary, attaches itself to God and often says that whatever is not God's is nothing to it; and as through a motive of charity it takes part in things committed to it, so through humility and self-denial it willingly gives up all share in those which are denied it.... I am diffident and have no self-confidence, and therefore I wish to be allowed to live in a way congenial to this disposition; any one can see that this is not according to the spirit.... But, although I am naturally timorous and retiring, I desire to try and overcome these traits of character and to fulfil all the requirements of the charge imposed upon me by obedience; who does not see that this is to live according to the spirit?

Hence, as I have said before, my dear daughter, to live according to the spirit is to have our actions, our words and our thoughts such as the spirit of God would require of us. When I say thoughts, I of course mean voluntary thoughts. I am sad, says some one, consequently I shall not speak; magpies and parrots do the same: I am sad, but as charity requires me to speak, I shall do so; spiritual persons act thus: I am slighted and I get angry: so do peacocks and monkeys. I am slighted and I rejoice thereat: that is what the Apostles did."

In fine, to live according to the spirit is to do in all circumstances and on all occasions whatever faith, hope and charity demand of us, without even waiting to consider if we are or are not influenced by our natural disposition. (The Imitation of Christ, B. III., Ch. LIV.)*

10. Generally speaking it is only after a long and painful struggle that one succeeds in climbing the mount of perfection. There are some statues, says Saint Francis de Sales, that it has cost the artist thirty years' labor to perfect. Now the perfecting of a soul is a much more difficult work. We must therefore set about it with tranquillity, patience and confidence in God. We shall always obtain what we wish soon enough if we obtain it at the time God pleases to grant it.

PART THIRD.
SOCIAL LIFE.

XVIII.
CHARITY.

By this shall all men know that ye are my disciples, if ye have love one for another. (St. John, c. XIII., v. 35.)

He who saith he is in the light, and hateth his brother, he is in darkness even until now. (St. John, Ep. I., c. II., v. 9.)

1. Our divine Lord has said that His disciples should be known by their love one for another. This christian virtue of charity makes us love our neighbor in God, the creature for the sake of the Creator. Love of God, love of our neighbor,—these virtues are two branches springing from the same trunk and having but one and the same root.

2. Assist your brethren in their needs whenever you can. However, you should always be careful to consult the laws of prudence in this matter and to be guided by your means and position. Supply by a desire to do good for the material aid you are unable to give.

3. When your neighbor offends you he does not cease on that account to be the creature and the image of God; therefore the christian motive you have for loving him still exists. He is not, perhaps, worthy of pardon, but has not our Saviour Jesus Christ, who so often has forgiven you much more grievous offences, merited it for him?

4. Observe, however, that we can scarcely avoid feeling some repugnance for those who have offended us, but to feel

and to consent are two distinct and widely different things, as we have already said. When religion commands us to love our enemies, the commandment is addressed to the superior portion of the soul, the will, not to the inferior portion in which reside the carnal affections that follow the natural inclinations. In a word, when we speak of charity the question is not of that human friendship which we feel for those who are naturally pleasing to us, a sentiment wherein we seek merely our own satisfaction and which therefore has nothing in common with charity.

*"Charity makes us love God above all things; and our neighbor as ourselves with a love not sensual, not natural, not interested, but pure, strong and unwavering, and having its foundation in God.... A person is extremely sweet and agreeable and I love her tenderly: or, she loves me well and does much to oblige me, and on that account I love her in return. Who does not see that this affection is according to the senses and the flesh? For animals that have no soul but only a body and senses, love those who are good and gentle and kind to them. Then there is another person who is brusque and uncivil, but apart from this is really devout and even desirous of becoming gentler and more courteous: consequently, not for any gratification she affords me, or for any self-interested motive whatever, but solely for the good pleasure of God, I talk to her, aid her, love her. This is the virtue of charity indeed, for nature has no share in it."—Saint Francis de Sales. (Read St. Luke, C. VI., vv. 32-33-34.)

The literal and exact fulfilment of the evangelical precept is often found impracticable. How, we say, is it possible to have for all men indiscriminately that extreme sensibility we feel for everything that touches us individually, that constant solicitude for our spiritual or temporal interests, that delicacy of feeling that we reserve for ourselves and for certain objects specially dear to us?—And yet it is literally au pied de la lettre, that our Lord's precept should be observed. What then is to be done? An answer will be found in the following passage from Fénelon, and we shall see that it is not a question of exaggerating the love of one's neighbor, but of moderating self-love, and thus making both the one and the other alike subordinate to the love of God:

"To love our neighbor as ourselves does not mean that we should have for him that intense feeling of affection that we have for ourselves, but simply that we wish for him, and from the motive of charity, what we wish for ourselves. Pure and genuine love, love having for its sole end the object beloved, should be reserved for God alone, and to bestow it elsewhere is a violation of a divine right."*

5. But although it is forbidden us to show hatred or to entertain it voluntarily against the wicked and those who have offended us, this is not meant to prevent us from defending ourselves or taking such precautions against them as prudence suggests. Christian charity obliges and disposes us to love our enemies and to be good to them when there is occasion to do so; but it should not carry us so far as to protect the wicked, nor leave us without defence against their aggressiveness. It allows us to be vigilant in guarding against their encroachments, and to take precautions against their machinations.

6. Always be ready and willing to excuse the faults of your neighbor, and never put an unfavorable interpretation upon his actions. The same action, says Saint Francis de Sales, may be looked upon under many different aspects: a charitable person will ever suppose the best, an uncharitable one will just as certainly choose the worst.

"Do not weigh so carefully the sayings and doings of others, but let your thought of them be simple and good, kindly and affectionate. You should not exact of your neighbor greater perfection than of yourself, nor be surprised at the diversity of imperfections; for an imperfection is not more an imperfection from the fact that it is extravagant and peculiar."

7. It is very difficult for a good christian to become really guilty of rash judgment, in the true sense of the word,— which is that, without just reasons or sufficient grounds he forms and pronounces in his own mind in a positive manner a condemnation of his neighbor. The grave sin of rash judgment is frequently confounded with suspicion or even simple distrust, which may be justifiable on much slighter grounds.

8. Suspicion is permissible when it has for its aim measures of just prudence; charity forbids gratuitously malevolent thoughts, but not vigilance and precaution.

9. Suspicion is not only permissible, but it is at times an important duty for those who are charged with the direction and guardianship of others. Thus it is a positive obligation for a father in regard to his children, and for a master in regard to his servants, whenever there is occasion to correct some vice they know exists, or to prevent some fault they have reasonable cause to fear.

10. As to simple mistrust, which should not be confused with suspicion, it is only an involuntary and purely passive condition, to which we may be more or less inclined by our natural disposition without our free-will being at all involved. Mistrust, suspicion, rash judgment are then three distinct and very different things, and we should be careful not to confound them.

XIX.
ZEAL.

But if you have bitter zeal, and there be contentions in your heart, glory not, and be not liars against the truth: for this is not wisdom descending from above, but earthly, sensual, diabolical. (St. James, Cath. Ep., c. III, vv. 14 and 15.)

For the anger of man worketh not the justice of God. (St. James, Cath. Ep., c. I., v. 20.)

1. Zeal for the salvation of souls is a sublime virtue, and yet how many errors and sins are every day committed in its name! Evil is never done more effectually and with greater security, says Saint Francis de Sales, than when one does it believing he is working for the glory of God.

2. The saints themselves can be mistaken in this delicate matter. We see a proof of this in the incident related of the Apostles Saint James and Saint John; for our Lord reprimanded them for asking Him to cause fire from heaven to fall upon the Samaritans.(20)

3. Acts of zeal are like coins the stamp upon which it is necessary to examine attentively, as there are more counterfeits than good ones. Zeal to be pure should be accompanied with very great humility, for it is of all virtues the one into which self-love most easily glides. When it does so, zeal is apt to become imprudent, presumptuous, unjust, bitter. Let us consider these characteristics in detail, viewing them, for the sake of greater clearness, in their practical bearings.

4. In every home there grows some thorn, something, in other words, that needs correction; for the best soil is seldom without its noxious weed. Imprudent zeal, by seeking awk-

wardly to pluck out the thorn, often succeeds only in plunging it farther in, thus rendering the wound deeper and more painful. In such a case it is essential to act with reflection and great prudence. There is a time to speak and a time to be silent, says the Holy Spirit.(21) Prudent zeal is silent when it realizes that to be so is less hurtful than to speak.

5. Some persons are even presumptuous enough in their mistaken zeal to meddle in the domestic affairs of strange families, blaming, counselling, attempting to reform without measure or discretion, thus causing an evil much greater than the one they wish to correct. Let us employ the activity of our zeal in our own reformation, says Saint Bernard, and pray humbly for that of others. It is great presumption on our part thus to assume the rôle of apostles when we are not as yet even good and faithful disciples. Not that you should be by any means indifferent to the salvation of souls: on the contrary you must wish it most ardently, but do not undertake to effect it except with great prudence, humility and diffidence in self.

6. Again, there are pious persons whose zeal consists in wishing to make everybody adopt their particular practices of devotion. Such a one, if she have a special attraction for meditating on the Passion of our divine Lord or for visiting the Blessed Sacrament, would like to oblige every one, under pain of reprobation, to pass long hours prostrate before the crucifix or the tabernacle. Another who is especially devoted to visiting the poor and the sick and to the other works of corporal mercy, acknowledges no piety apart from these excellent practices. Now, this is not an enlightened zeal. Martha and Mary were sisters, says Saint Augustine, but they have not a like office: one acts, the other contemplates. If both had passed the day in contemplation, no one

would have prepared a repast for their divine Master; if both had been employed in this material work, there would have been no one to listen to His words and garner up His divine lessons. The same thing may be said of other good works. In choosing among them each person should follow the inspirations of God's grace, and these are very varied. The eye that sees but hears not, must neither envy nor blame the ear that hears but sees not. Omnis spiritus laudet Dominum: let every spirit praise the Lord, says the royal prophet.(22)

7. Bear well in mind that the zeal which would lead you to undertake works not in conformity with your position, however good and useful they may be in themselves, is always a false one. This is especially true if such cause us interior trouble or annoyance; for the holiest things are infallibly displeasing to God when they do not accord with the duties of our state of life.

8. Saint Paul condemned in strong terms those Christians who showed a too exclusive preference for their spiritual masters; some admitting as truth only what came from the mouth of Peter, others acknowledging none save Paul, and others again none but Apollo. What! said he to them, is not Jesus Christ the same for all of you! Is it then Paul who was crucified for you? Is it in his name you were baptized?(23) This culpable weakness is often reproduced in our day. Persons otherwise pious carry to excess the esteem and affection they have for their spiritual directors, exalt without measure their wisdom and holiness, and do not scruple to depreciate all others. God alone knows the true value of each human being, and we have not the scales of the sanctuary to weigh and compare the respective wisdom and sanctity of this and that person. If you have a good confessor, thank God and try to render his wisdom useful to you by your

docility in allowing yourself to be guided; but do not assume that nobody else has as good a one. To depreciate the merits of some in order to exalt those of others at their expense is a sort of slander, that ought to be all the more feared because it is generally so little recognized.

9. "If your zeal is bitter," says Saint James, "it is not wisdom descending from on high, but earthly, sensual, diabolical."(24) These words of an Apostle should furnish matter of reflection for those persons who, whilst making profession of piety, are so prone to irritability, so harsh and rude in their manners and language, that they might be taken for angels in church and for demons elsewhere.

10. The value and utility of zeal are in proportion to its tolerance and amiability. True zeal is the offspring of charity: it should, then, resemble its mother and show itself like to her in all things. "Charity," says Saint Paul, "is patient, is kind, is not ambitious and seeketh not her own."(25)

"You should not only be devout and love devotion, but you ought to make your piety useful, agreeable and charming to everybody. The sick will like your spirituality if they are lovingly consoled by it; your family, if they find that it makes you more thoughtful of their welfare, gentler in every day affairs, more amiable in reproving, and so on; your husband, if he sees that in proportion as your devotion increases you become more cordial and tender in your affection for him; your relations and friends, if they find you more forbearing, and more ready to comply with their wishes, should these not be contrary to God's will. Briefly, you must try as far as possible to make your devotion attractive to others; that is true zeal."—Saint Francis de Sales.

11. Never allow your zeal to make you over eager to correct others, says the same Saint; and when you must do it remember that the most important thing to consider is the choice of the moment. A caution deferred can be given another time: one given inopportunely is not only fruitless, but moreover paralyses beforehand all the good that might have subsequently been done.

12. Be zealous, therefore, ardently zealous for the salvation of your neighbor, and to further it make use of whatever means God has placed in your power; but do not exceed these limits nor disquiet yourself about the good you are unable to do, for God can accomplish it through others. In conclusion, zeal, according to the teachings of the Fathers of the Church, should always have truth for its foundation, indulgence for its companion, mildness for its guide, prudence for its counsellor and director.

"I must look upon whatever presents itself each day to be done, in the order of Divine Providence, as the work God wishes me to do, and apply myself to it in a manner worthy of Him, that is with exactness and tranquillity. I shall neglect nothing, be anxious about nothing; as it is dangerous either to do God's work negligently or to appropriate it to one's self through self-love and false zeal. When our actions are prompted by our own inclinations, we do them badly, and are pretentious, restless, and anxious to succeed. The glory of God is the pretext that hides the illusion. Self-love disguised as zeal grieves and frets if it cannot succeed. O my God! give me the grace to be faithful in action, indifferent to success. My part is to will what Thou willest and to keep myself recollected in Thee amidst all my occupations: Thine it is to give to my feeble efforts such fruit as shall please Thee,—none if Thou so wishest."—Fénelon.

XX.
MEEKNESS.

Blessed are the meek for they shall possess the land. (S. Matth., c. V., v. 4.)

Learn of me because I am meek. (St. Matthew, c. XI., v. 29.)

1. Our Lord offers us in His Divine Person a model of all the virtues. Meekness, however, is the one that He seems to have wished more particularly to propose for our imitation since He said: "Learn of Me for I am meek and humble of heart."

2. Try, therefore, to acquire and always preserve in your soul this christian virtue and to make all your exterior actions correspond with it. I do not say that you should never have the slightest feeling of irritation, as that would be to expect an impossibility; but you should be attentive to repress these movements and never yield to them voluntarily. It is natural for man to be often assailed by anger, says Saint Jerome, but it is peculiar to the Christian not to allow himself to be overcome by it.

3. A Christian, says Saint Bernard, who has no one at hand who gives him occasion to suffer, should seek such a person eagerly and buy him at any price, that he may have opportunity to practice meekness and patience. If you are not disposed to go to this expense, at least profit of whatever opportunities divine Providence has given you gratuitously, that you may accustom yourself to the exercise of these two inestimable virtues.

4. An excellent rule to follow is to make a compact with your tongue such as Saint Francis de Sales did with his,

namely, that the tongue remain silent whenever the feelings are irritated. Otherwise you will begin to speak with the sincere resolution to keep within the bounds of moderation and prudence, but you will never succeed in so doing, because the bridle once loosened you will invariably be carried farther than you wished. Reprimand from an angry man can do no good. Reproof is a moral remedy: how would it be possible for you to select and administer this remedy with discernment and prudence, when you yourself are ill and stand in need of both medicine and physician? Wait therefore until your soul is at peace, and when you have been restored to calmness you can speak advantageously. Even when it is your positive duty to administer a rebuke, defer it if possible until free from excitement, remembering that to have a salutary effect both he who gives it and he who receives it must be calm. Without this precaution the remedy will only aggravate the disease.

5. When obliged to reprove the fault of another, never fail to pray that God will speak to the person's heart whilst your words are sounding in his ears.

6. Observe, however, with Saint Gregory the Great and Saint Thomas, that if those it is your duty to correct abuse your mildness and considerateness, you are then justified in repressing their boldness with vigor and firmness. "Speak to the fool," says the Holy Spirit, "the language that his folly renders necessary, that he may not continue wise in his own eyes."(26) I repeat it: reproof is a remedy, and a remedy must be chosen and proportioned according to the nature and gravity of the evil.

XXI.
CONVERSATION.

Neither do men light a candle and put it under a bushel, but upon a candlestick, that it may give light to all who are in a house.

Let your light so shine before men that they may see your good works, and glorify your Father who is in heaven. (St. Matthew, c. V., vv. 15-16.)

Contend not in words, for it is to no profit, but to the subversion of the hearers. (St. Paul, II Tim., c. II., v. 14.)

1. Conversation should be marked by a gentle and devout pleasantness, and your manner when engaged in it, ought to be equable, composed and gracious. Mildness and cheerfulness make devotion and those who practice it attractive to others. The holy abbot Saint Anthony, notwithstanding the extraordinary austerities of his penitential life, always showed such a smiling countenance that no one could look at him without pleasure.

2. We should be neither too talkative nor too silent,—it is as necessary to avoid one extreme as the other. By speaking too much we expose ourselves to a thousand dangers, so well known that they need not be mentioned in detail: by not speaking enough we are apt to be a restraint upon others, as it makes it seem as though we did not relish their conversation, or wished to impress them with our superiority.

*"Take great care not to be too critical of conversations in which the rules of devotion are not very exactly observed. In all such matters it is necessary that charity should govern

114

and enlighten us in order to make us accede to the wishes of our neighbor in whatever is not in any way contrary to the commandments of God."—Saint Francis de Sales.*

3. Do not conclude from this that it is necessary to count your words, as it were, so as to keep your conversation within the proper limits. This would be as puerile a scruple as counting one's steps when walking. A holy spirit of liberty should dominate our conversations and serve to instil into them a gentle and moderate gaiety.

4. If you hear some evil spoken of your neighbor do not immediately become alarmed, as the matter may be true and quite public without your having been aware of it. Should you be quite certain that there is calumny or slander in the report, either because the evil told was false or exaggerated or because it was not publicly known, then, according to the place, the circumstances and your relations towards those present, say with moderation what appears most fitting to justify or excuse your neighbor. Or you may try to turn the conversation into other channels, or simply be content to show your disapprobation by an expressive silence. Remember, for the peace of your conscience, that one does not share in the sin of slander unless he give some mark of approbation or encouragement to the person who is guilty of it.

5. Do not imitate those who are scrupulous enough to imagine that charity obliges them to undertake the defence of every evil mentioned in their presence and to become the self-appointed advocates of whoever it may be that has deserved censure. That which is really wrong cannot be justified, and no one should attempt the fruitless task: and as to the guilty, those who may do harm either through the scandal of their example or the wickedness of their doctrines, it is right that

they should be shunned and openly denounced. "To cry out wolf, wolf," says Saint Francis de Sales, "is kindness to the sheep."

6. The regard we owe our neighbor does not bind us to a politeness that might be construed as an approval or encouragement of his vicious habits. Hence if it happen that you hear an equivocal jest, a witticism slurring at religion or morals, or anything else that really offends against propriety, be careful not to give, through cowardice and in spite of your conscience, any mark of approbation, were it only by one of those half smiles that are often accorded unwillingly and afterwards regretted. Flattery, even in the eyes of the world, is one of the most debasing of falsehoods. Not even in the presence of the greatest earthly dignitaries, will an honest, upright man sanction with his mouth that which he condemns in his heart. He who sacrifices to vice the rights of truth not only acts unlike a christian, but renders himself unworthy the name of man.

7. In small social gatherings try to make yourself agreeable to everybody present and to show to each some little mark of attention, if you can do so without affectation. This may be done either by directly addressing the person or by making a remark that you know will give him occasion to speak of his own accord,—draw him out, as the saying is. It was by the charm and urbanity of his conversation that Saint Francis de Sales prepared the way for the conversion of numbers of heretics and sinners, and by imitating him you will contribute towards making piety in the world more attractive. In regard to priests you should always testify your respect for the sacerdotal dignity quite independently of the individual.

8. Disputes, sarcasm, bitter language, and intolerance for

dissenting opinions, are the scourges of conversation.

9. Although this adage comes to us from a pagan philosopher, we might profitably bear it always in mind: "In conversation we should show deference to our superiors, affability to our equals, and benevolence to our inferiors."

10. Generally speaking, it is wrong for those whom God does not call to abandon the world, to seclude themselves entirely and to shun all society suited to their position in life. God, who is the source of all virtue, is likewise the author of human society. Let the wicked hide themselves if they will, their absence is no loss to the world; but good people make themselves useful merely by being seen. It is well, moreover, the world should know that in order to practice the teachings of the Gospel it is not necessary to bury one's self in the desert; and that those who live for the Creator can likewise live with the creatures whom He has made according to His own image and likeness. Well, again, to show that a devout life is neither sad nor austere, but simple, sweet and easy; that far from being for those in the world an impediment to social relations, it facilitates, perfects and sanctifies such; that the disciples of Jesus Christ can, without becoming worldlings, live in the world; and that, in fine, the Gospel is the sovereign code of perfection for persons in society as well as for those who have renounced the world.

*Fénelon, who perhaps had even greater occasion than Saint Francis de Sales to teach men of the world how to lead a Christian life in society, wrote as follows to a person at court:

"You ought not to feel worried, it seems to me, in regard to those diversions in which you cannot avoid taking part. I

117

know there are those who think it necessary that one should lament about everything, and restrain himself continually by trying to excite disgust for the amusements in which he must participate. As for me, I acknowledge that I cannot reconcile myself to this severity. I prefer something more simple and I believe that God, too, likes it better. When amusements are innocent in themselves and we enter into them to conform to the customs of the state of life in which Providence has placed us, then I believe they are perfectly lawful. It is enough to keep within the bounds of moderation and to remember God's presence. A dry, reserved manner, conduct not thoroughly ingenuous and obliging, only serve to give a false idea of piety to men of the world who are already too much prejudiced against it, believing that a spiritual life cannot be otherwise than gloomy and morose."*

11. If all confessors agreed in instilling these maxims, which are as important as they are true, many persons who now keep themselves in absolute seclusion and live in a sad and dreary solitude would remain in society to the edification of their neighbor and the great advantage of religion. The world would thus be disabused of its unjust prejudices against a devout life and those who have embraced it.

12. Never remain idle except during the time you have allotted to rest or recreation. Idleness begets lassitude, disposes to evil speaking and gives occasion to the most dangerous temptations.

XXII.
DRESS.

Women also in decent apparel, adorning themselves with modesty and sobriety. (St. Paul, I. Tim., c. II., v. 9.)

1. Clothing is worn for a threefold object: to observe the laws of propriety, to protect our bodies from the inclemency of the weather, and, finally, to adorn them, as Saint Paul says, with modesty and sobriety. This third end is, as you see, not less legitimate than the other two, provided you are careful to make it accord with them by confining it within proper limits and not permitting it to be the only one to which you attach any importance, so that neither health nor propriety be sacrificed to personal appearance.

2. External ornamentation should correspond with each one's condition in life. A just proportion in this matter, says Saint Thomas, is an offshoot of the virtues of uprightness and sincerity, for there is a sort of untruthfulness in appearing in garments that are calculated to give a wrong impression as to the position in which God has placed us in this world.

3. Be equally careful, then, to avoid over-nicety and carelessness in respect to matters of toilet. Excessive nicety sins against moderation and christian simplicity; negligence, against the order that should govern certain externals in human society. This order requires that each one's material life, and accordingly his attire which is a part of it, be suitable to his rank and condition; that Esther be clad as a queen, Judith as a woman of wealth and position, Agar as a bond-woman.

5. I shall not speak of immodest dress, for these instruc-

tions being intended for pious persons or for those who are endeavoring to become such, it would seem unnecessary. Nevertheless, as some false and pernicious ideas on this subject prevail in the world and lead into error souls desirous to do right, here are some fundamental principles that can serve you as a rule and save you from similar mistakes.

5. A generally admitted custom can and even should be followed in all indifferent matters; but no custom, however universal it may be, can ever have the power to change the nature and essence of things or render allowable that which is in itself indecent and immodest. Were it otherwise, many sins could be justified by the sanction they receive in fashionable society. Remember, therefore, that the sin of others can never in the sight of God authorize yours, and that where it is the fashion to sin it is likewise the fashion to go to hell. Hence it rests with yourself whether you prefer to be saved with the few or to be damned with the many.

XXIII.
HUMAN RESPECT.

I will pay my vows to the Lord before all his people.... Lo, I will not restrain my lips.... I have not concealed thy mercy and thy truth from a great council. (Psalms CXV. and XXX-IX.)

That which you hear in the ear, preach ye upon the house-tops.... Whosoever shall confess me before men, I will also confess him before my Father who is in heaven. (St. Matthew, c. X., vv. 27-32.)

1. Charity towards your neighbor, tolerance for his opinions, indulgence for his defects, compassion for his errors, yes; but no cowardly and guilty concessions to human respect. Never allow fear of the ridicule or contempt of men to make you blush for your faith.

2. We are not even forbidden to call one human weakness to the assistance of another that is contrary to it: men do not like to contradict themselves, and they dread to be considered fickle. Well, then, in order that no person may be ignorant of the fact that you are a christian, once for all boldly confess your faith and your firm resolve to practise it, and let it be known that in all your actions your sole desire is to seek the glory of God and the good of your neighbor. Let this profession be made upon occasion in a gentle and modest manner, but firmly and positively; and you will find that subsequently it will be much easier for you to continue what you have thus courageously begun. (Read Chapters I. and II., IVth Part of the Introduction to a Devout Life.)

XXIV.
RESOLUTIONS.

Long-standing custom will make resistance, but by a better habit shall it be subdued. (Imitation, B. III., c. XII.)

To him who shall overcome, I will grant to sit with me in my throne, as I also have overcome. (Apocalypse, c. III., v. 21.)

1. We should not undertake to perfect ourselves upon all points at once; resolutions as to details ought to be made and carried out one by one, directing them first against our predominant passion.

2. By a predominant passion we mean the source of that sin to which we oftenest yield and from which spring the greater number of our faults.

3. In order to attack it successfully it is essential to make use of strategy. It must be approached little by little, besieged with great caution as if it were the stronghold of an enemy, and the outposts taken one after another.
4. For example, if your ruling passion be anger, simply propose to yourself in the beginning never to speak when you feel irritated. Renew this resolution two or three times during the day and ask God's pardon for every time you have failed against it.

5. When the results of this first resolution shall have become a habit, so that you no longer have any difficulty in keeping it, you can take a step forward. Propose, for instance, to repress promptly every thought capable of agitating you, or of arousing interior anger; afterwards you can adopt the practice of meeting without annoyance persons who are naturally

repugnant to you; then of being able to treat with especial kindness those of whom you have reason to complain. Finally, you will learn to see in all things, even in those most painful to nature, the will of God offering you opportunities to acquire merit; and in those who cause you suffering, only the instruments of this same merciful providence. You will then no longer think of repulsing or bewailing them, but will bless and thank your divine Saviour for having chosen you to bear with Him the burden of His cross, and for deigning to hold to your lips the precious chalice of His passion.

6. Some saints recommend us to make an act of hope or love or to perform some act of mortification when we discover that we have failed to keep our resolutions. This practice is good, but if you adopt it do not consider it of obligation nor bind yourself so strictly to it as to suppose you have committed a sin when you neglect it.

7. It is by this progressive method that you can at length succeed in entirely overcoming your passions, and will be able to acquire the virtues you lack. Always begin with what is easiest. Choose at first external acts over which the will has greater control, and in time you can advance from these, little by little, to the most interior and difficult details of the spiritual life.

8. Resolutions of too general a character, such as, for example, to be always moderate in speech, always patient, chaste, peaceable and the like, ordinarily do not amount to much and sometimes to nothing at all.

9. To undertake little at a time, and to pursue this little with perseverance until one has by degrees brought it to perfection, is a common rule of human prudence. The saints

particularly recommend us to apply it to the subject of our resolutions.

XXV.
CONCLUSION.

But continue thou in the things which thou hast learned and which have been committed to thee; knowing of whom thou hast learned them. (St. Paul, II Tim., c. III., v. 14.)

1. The writer of these instructions makes no pretension to have derived them from his own wisdom. The material was furnished him by the greatest saints and the most eminent doctors of the Church. You can therefore believe in them with great confidence, follow them without fear and adopt them as a safe and reliable guide in your spiritual life.

2. If you try to regulate your practice by making personal and indiscriminate application of everything you find in sermons and books you will never be at rest. One draws you to the right, the other to the left, says Saint Francis de Sales: doctrine is one, but its applications are many, and they vary according to time, place and person. Besides, those who speak to a hardened multitude, from whom they cannot get even a little without exacting a great deal, insist vehemently upon the subject with which they wish to impress their hearers and for the time being appear to forget everything else. If they preach on mortification of the senses, fasting, or any other penitential work, they fail to explain the proper manner of practising it, the limits that should not usually be exceeded and the circumstances under which we can and should refrain from it. This is due to the fact that the cowardly and the lukewarm, whom it is more necessary to excite than to restrain, will take from these instructions only just what is suitable for them. Now as these form the majority, it is for them above all that it is necessary to speak.

3. It would then be better for you individually, without lessening your respect and esteem for books of devotion and for preachers animated by the spirit of God, to confine yourself as far as practice is concerned to the advice of your director and to the teachings of the saints as presented in this little volume.

4. Recall what has been already said, that Saint Francis de Sales counsels you to select your spiritual guide from among ten thousand, and to allow yourself subsequently to be entirely directed by him as though he were an angel come down from heaven to conduct you there.

5. Without this rule of firm and confident obedience, books and sermons and all that is said and written for the multitude, will become for you a source of fatiguing inquietude, and of doubts and fears, owing to the fact that you will try to assimilate things which were not intended for you.

6. Remember, moreover, the pleasant saying of Saint Philip de Neri,—namely, that he had a special predilection for those books the authors of which had a name beginning with the letter S.; that is to say, the works of the saints, because he supposed them to be more illumined by heavenly wisdom.

Now, in observing these instructions you will have for guide and director not the poor sinner who has compiled them for the glory of God and the good of souls, but Saint Augustine, Saint Thomas, Saint Philip de Neri and especially Saint Francis de Sales, in whom the Church recognizes and admires such exalted sanctity, profound wisdom, and rare experience in the direction of souls. These are the three eminent qualities requisite to constitute a great doctor in the Catholic Church, and to form the safest and the most enlightened guide for those who wish to be his disciples.

ADDITIONS.
FINAL ADVICE IN REGARD
TO HOLY COMMUNION.

A cause of frequent error and trouble, particularly in regard to Holy Communion, is that feelings are confused with acts of the will. The faculty of willing is the only one we possess as our own, the only one we can use freely and at all times. Hence it follows that it is by the will alone that we can in reality acquire merit or commit sin. The natural virtues are gratuitous gifts of God. The world is right in esteeming them for they come from Him, but it errs when it esteems them exclusively for they do not of themselves give us any title to heaven. God has placed them at the disposal of our will as means to an end, and we can make a good or bad use of them just as we can of all God's other gifts. We may be deprived of these natural virtues and live by the will alone, spiritually dry and devoid of sentiment, and yet in a state of intimate union with God.

This explanation is intended to reassure such persons as are disposed to feel anxious when they find nothing in their hearts to correspond with the effusions of sensible love with which books of devotion abound in the preparation for Holy Communion. These usually make the mistake of taking for granted the invariable existence of sentiment, and of addressing it exclusively. How many souls do we not see who in consequence grow alarmed about their condition, believing they are devoid of grace notwithstanding their firm will to shun sin and to please God! They should, however, not give way to anxiety, nor exhaust themselves by vain efforts to excite in their hearts a sensibility that God has not given them. When He has granted us this gift we owe Him homage for it as for all others; but God only requires that each of His creatures should render an account of what he has received, and free-will is the one thing that has been accorded indiscriminately to all men. Thus we find Saint Francis de Sales, who possessed in such a high degree sensible love of God and all the natural virtues, making this positive declaration: "The greatest proof we can have in this life that we are in the grace of God, is not sensible love of Him, but the firm resolution never to consent to any sin great or small."

Pious persons can make use of the following prayers with profit when they are habitually or accidentally in the condition described above. They will then see how the will alone, without the aid of feeling, can produce acts of all the christian virtues.

Act of Confidence.
I will go unto the altar of God. (Ps. XLII.)

It is obedience, O my God! that leads me to Thy Holy Table: the tender words by which Thou hast invited us would not have sufficed to draw me, for in the troubled state of my soul I cannot be sure they are addressed to me. Misery and infirmity are claims for admission to Thy Feast, but nothing can dispense from the nuptial garment. Therefore when I turn my eyes on myself, after having raised them to Thee, I doubt, I hesitate, I tremble; for if I go from Thee I flee from life, and if I approach unworthily, to my other sins I add the crime of sacrilege.(27) But Thy merciful wisdom, O my God, whilst foreseeing our every need, has foreseen all our weaknesses and has prepared helps for us against both presumption and distrust. For if Thou hast not willed that, certain of Thy grace, we should ever advance with the assurance of the Pharisee and say like him: I come to the altar of the Lord because I know I am just in His eyes: neither hast

Thou permitted that a sacrament of love should become for us a torture and an unavoidable snare. I therefore obey, O my God, and in the darkness that envelops me I wish to follow implicitly the guidance of him whom Thou hast appointed to lead me to Thee. I shall approach the Holy Table without wishing for any other warrant than the words spoken by my confessor, or rather by Thee: You may receive Holy Communion. I accept, O my God!—be it a well merited punishment or a salutary trial,—this privation of light and sensible devotion, this coldness and distraction, which accompany me even into Thy presence when all the faculties of my soul should be absorbed and confounded in sentiments of adoration and of love. Faith, hope and charity seem to be extinct in my heart, but I know that Thou never withdrawest these virtues when we do not voluntarily renounce them.

Act of Faith.

Notwithstanding, then, the doubts that cross my mind, I wish to believe, O my God! and I do believe all that Thy holy Church has taught me. I have not forgotten that brilliant light of Faith which Thou didst cause to illumine my soul in the days of mercy in order that the precious remembrance of it should serve me as support in the days of trial and temptation.

Act of Hope.

In spite of these vague fears that seem to extinguish hope within my soul, I know that although Thou art the mighty and strong God before whom the cherubim veil themselves with their wings, the just and all-seeing God who discovers blemishes in the purest souls, still Thou wishest to be in the most Holy Sacrament only the Victim whose Blood effaces the sins of the world; the Good Shepherd who hastens after the strayed sheep and carries it tenderly and unreproachfully back to the fold; the divine Mediator who comes not to judge but to save.(28) All this I know, O my God! and therefore I hope.

Act of Love.
Notwithstanding the coldness and insensibility that benumb my soul, I know that I love Thee, O my God! since my will prefers Thy service to all the joys of this world, since Thy grace is the sole good to which I aspire, and because I suffer so much by reason of my lack of sensible love for Thee.

Act of Desire.
No, I am not indifferent, Thou knowest, O my God! that I am not indifferent to this Most Holy Sacrament which I approach unmoved by any sensible feeling: for Thou seest that although I find in Holy Communion neither relish nor consolation, I would yet make any sacrifice in order to receive it.

Act of Contrition.
I feel neither hatred nor horror of sins to which the world does not attach shame and contempt; I experience no sensible sorrow for the sins I have committed, but I know, O my God! that, with the assistance of Thy grace, my will denounces them, for I am resolved to commit them no more. I have taken this resolution because sin displeases Thee and because all that swerves from eternal order is abhorrent to Thy infinite sanctity. I believe, then, that I am contrite, O my God! because I believe in Thy promises, and if Thou dost not always grant us the consolation of realizing our contrition, Thou wilt never refuse its justifying virtue to those who humbly implore it; and this I do.

No, my God, I shall not pray Thee to grant me sensible enjoyment, not even that of Thy spiritual gifts: what I implore of Thy grace is to keep my will ever turned towards Thee and never to permit it to fall or wander anew on the earth.

Lord! into Thy hands I commend my spirit.

(Read The Imitation, Chapters IV., XIV., XV. of B. IV.; and Chapters XXV., XLVIII and LII of B. III.)

If you have an ardent desire for the sensible love of God, a desire that cannot but be pleasing to Him provided you are at the same time resigned to be deprived of it, remember that according to Saint John Chrysostom it can be obtained only by fidelity to prayer. God wishes, says the Saint, to make us realize by experience that we cannot have His love but from Himself, and that this love, which is the true happiness of our souls, is not to be acquired by the reflections of our minds or the natural efforts of our hearts, but by the gratu- itous infusion of the Holy Ghost. Yes, this love is so great a good that God wishes to be the sole dispenser of it: He bestows it only in proportion as we ask it of Him, and ordi- narily makes us wait for some time before He grants it.

There are few prayers better calculated to dispose the soul to receive this great grace than the XVI. and XVII. chapters of the IVth. Book, and XXI. and XXXIV. of the IIId. Book of The Imitation.

For thanksgiving after Communion, read Chapters XXXIV., V., XXI., II. and X. of the III. Book of The Imitation.

Footnotes

(1)Saint Paul, I. Cor. x., 13, says: ... God is faithful, Who will not suffer you to be tempted above what you are able: but will even make with temptation an issue, that you may be able to bear it.

(2)The Chevalier du Chambon de Mésilliac, who translated this little work of P. Quadrupani's into French, inserted much additional matter, quotations for the most part from the same authorities frequently cited by the Italian author. These selections he placed at the end of each Instruction under the title of "Additions." The English translator has changed this arrangement into one which seems more convenient and better calculated to maintain the connection of ideas. Therefore the extracts chosen by the French translator are here inserted in the body of the text, immediately following the paragraphs which suggested them, and are marked by asterisks to distinguish them from the original matter.

(3)St. Francis de Sales.

(4)Proverbs, XXX, 21-23: "By three things is the earth disturbed ... by a bondwoman, when she is heir to her mistress...."

(5)II. Cor., xii., 9.

(6)John, vi, 57.

(7)Matt. xi., 28.

(8)Saint Luke, c. V. vv. 8-10.

(9)Luke V., 32. Mark II., 17. Matthew IX., 13.

(10)Epist. St. Paul to the Hebrews.

(11)St. Paul to the Philippians, IV., 13.

(12)Matt. X., 30.

(13)Matt. X., 30:—Luke XII., 7.—"Blessed are they that mourn, for they shall be comforted."

(14)III Kings, C. XIX.

(15)Ecce in pace est amaritudo mea amarissima. (Isaias.)

(16)Saint Francis de Sales.

(17)See P. Rodriguez, S. J., Christian Perfection, C. I.

(18)Gen. I., 11.

(19)Psalm CL., 5. Let every spirit praise the Lord.

(20)Luke, IX., 54.

(21)Ecclesiastes III., 7.

(22)Ps. CL., 5.

(23)St. Paul, I Cor. I., 13.

(24)S. James, Cath. Ep. III., 14-15.

(25)S. Paul, I Cor. XIII., 4-5.

(26)Proverbs, XXVI., 5.

(27)Imitation, B. IV., c. VI.: "For if I do not appeal to Thee, I fly from life; and if I intrude myself unworthily I incur Thy displeasure."

(28)S. John, c. XII., v. 47: "For I came not to judge the world, but to save the world."

Made in the USA
Lexington, KY
28 January 2019